SO NOW YOU ARE A CHRISTIAN...

By Stephen W. Brown

WHERE THE ACTION IS
SO NOW YOU ARE A CHRISTIAN . . .

STEPHEN
W. BROWN

SO NOW YOU ARE A CHRISTIAN...

Fleming H. Revell Company
Old Tappan, New Jersey

Scripture quotations in this volume are from the
Revised Standard Version of the Bible.

The poem "Christ Has No Hands" is by Annie Johnson Flint.
Copyright. Reproduced by permission. Evangelical Publishers,
Toronto, Canada.

Library of Congress Cataloging in Publication Data

Brown, Stephen W
   So now you are a Christian . . .

   1. Christian life—Presbyterian authors. I. Title.
BV4501.2.B768   248′.48′51   70–186534
ISBN 0–8007–0520–3
ISBN 0–8007–0529–7 (pbk.)

TO my brothers and sisters
who make up the congregation of
First United Presbyterian Church of Quincy, Massachusetts,
and who are living illustrations
of that which is taught herein.

Contents

Introduction

One of the great facts of our time is that Christians all over the world are once again taking seriously the commandment of Jesus to make disciples. Joe Pagan and Jane Cynic have told these Christians to keep quiet. It would be much better, they say, if the Christians would go off somewhere to a nice, quiet, white church with pretty windows, and sing hymns. The old words have once again been dragged out and proclaimed with the old arrogance—fanaticism, fundamentalism, reactionism, intolerance, simplism, etc. They always worked before. Any combination of two or more were always enough to close the mouth of the most avid Jesus fan. But they didn't work this time, and Joe and Jane just don't understand. If they read this book, I hope they will.

However, I am not writing this book primarily for Joe Pagan and Jane Cynic. I am writing it for the new disciples of Jesus, my brothers and sisters, who have come into our family because other Christians refused to shut up—other Christians who cared enough to tell enough. It is important that you, my new brothers and sisters, have someone to tell you the truth about your new life. God has a wonderful and exciting place for you in our family, and He has an important task for you to perform. But before you go too far in that life, our Father has instructed some of us to assume the task of teachers (Ephesians 4:11) in the family. I am writing this book in an effort to fulfill that task.

The things I will say in this book are not just pious platitudes. They are principles that have come from Scripture, and have been tested in my life and the lives of hundreds of thousands of our brothers and sisters. It is important that you understand these principles just as it is important to know and understand the alphabet before you write a letter or read a book. It is my hope that you read and weigh the things said in this book, and that you read and weigh them under the guidance of the Holy Spirit. If you find truth here, it is also my hope that you will teach it to others who have come into our family because *you* cared enough to tell enough.

STEPHEN W. BROWN

SO NOW YOU ARE
A CHRISTIAN...

1

A Matter of Truth

If you continue in my word, you are truly my disciples, and you will know the truth, and the truth will make you free.　　　　JOHN 8:31, 32

We live in an age of tolerance. The axiom of this age is as follows: It doesn't matter what you believe as long as you believe in something, are sincere about it, and don't bother anyone with it. There are, say the spokesmen of the age, many ways to God. You take your way, and I will take mine, and we will all meet together someday before the throne of God. If your way makes you feel good, if it satisfies you, then it is right for you. If my way makes me feel good, if it satisfies me, then it is right for me. God, of course, smiles as we join hands and walk off into the sunset together.

There is only one thing wrong with that kind of tolerance: truth suffers. If truth suffers then people suffer. I'm from the mountains of western North Carolina, and in those mountains there are a lot of folks who still believe in old-fashioned methods of treating sickness. Some of those methods are good and they work, but some of them are useless and when used to the exclusion of modern medicine, keep people from getting well. If I should be visiting in the mountains and should develop a dangerous disease I hope the person who helps me isn't tolerant about medicine. You see, if I am really sick I don't want a spoonful of honey; I want a doctor who knows what he is doing and who is intolerant of folk medicine. If I should find myself in the hands of a doctor who said, "It really doesn't matter what medicine one uses so long as one believes that

13

it is the proper medicine," I might die. I like my doctors to be intolerant of folk medicine because I know there are certain truths which are important in medicine. (Honey doesn't cure cancer, and an herb will not heal a heart disease.) Men who play around with medical truth end up with a lot of corpses.

Recently a college student came to me who only a few weeks before had given her life to Christ. When she first became a Christian she had been excited and happy. But now this same young lady sat across from me in my study with tears streaming down her face. "Pastor," she said, "I don't know what has happened. When I first met Christ everything seemed so right. Now He isn't real anymore. I am sure that either I was kidding myself, or I have lost Christ." The problem with this young lady is fairly typical. She had misunderstood the fact that the Christian faith is not primarily a matter of feelings, but rather a matter of truth.

Because so many Christians misunderstand the faith at this point I thought it well to begin with some plain talk about truth. Everything in this book is based on the presuppositions you will find in this chapter. If the Christian isn't clear about truth, and what truth is, then his faith will die or become a dull habit. One of the great problems in the church in our time is that a lot of people who sit in the pews and serve on the boards are playing games. They are performing a service to humanity; they are working for a good cause; they are fulfilling their responsibility; they are doing the proper thing. But how few people in the church realize that they are under the constraint of truth! Time after time I have seen dead, empty, frustrated church members become alive, vibrant, joyful Christians because it dawned on them that all of the nice, pious, Christian things they had been talking about, and singing about, and praying about for years were really true.

John Morley, the British writer and statesman, and a man who could not see the truth of the Christian faith, once said, "If I believed that Jesus Christ was the Son of God and my Saviour, I would never write or talk anything else." He saw something most Christians never see! When you find out that all of the revolutionary things about which Jesus spoke are true, when you know that you *know* you know, when you have discovered the truth of the Bible, then faith is different, and alive, and dynamic because it is real.

You see, Christians have been, for some two thousand years now, telling the world that the God who rules and controls everything, the God who is omniscient, omnipresent and omnipotent has put His hand into man's history. We have been saying that this God has come to man in the form of His Son, that He walked man's dirty roads, suffered from man's dirty acts of violence, and took man's dirty sins to a cross. We have been saying that this Man died spread-eagled on crossbeams on the town garbage heap, and that His friends took His cold, dead cadaver down from that cross and placed it on a slab of stone in a borrowed tomb to rot as millions of cold, dead cadavers before had rotted. But we have also been telling the world that this dead Man didn't stay dead—He got up and walked and talked and told His disciples to spread the news. Not only that, we have been saying that when the last page of history has been turned, when all the historians are dead, this same Man will return to earth to judge the world, to establish His kingdom and to rule His people. We have been saying that all of man's history finds its meaning in these facts and that all men will be judged by their reaction to them.

If all of this is true then it is dynamite! If it is true, the man or woman who says he believes it and does nothing about it and does not get excited when he thinks about it, is either a fool or one who really doesn't believe it. If it is true, then Christians have gotten a hold on the most revolutionary, exciting and dynamic news in the history of the world. If it isn't true, mankind has been conned by the greatest con artist who ever spoke a smooth line.

It is then very important before we proceed any further that we examine the subject of truth as it relates to the Christian faith. Herewith are some observations. *First:* Truth is narrow and exclusive. Either the Christian faith is true or it isn't true; either God entered man's history in Jesus Christ or He didn't; either a dead Man walked or He didn't. One cannot have it both ways. For instance, I often hear people say, "I don't believe that Jesus was God or the Son of God, nor do I believe that He was unique, but I do believe that he was a good man, perhaps one of the greatest, and wisest and best men who

15

ever lived." Nonsense! Either Jesus was who He said He was or He was a liar and/or a psychopath. Certainly, if He was not what He said He was (i.e., God, the Giver of life, the Messiah, the vicarious suffering Servant of man, the Bearer of man's sin) then He could not be, by any stretch of the imagination, a good, wise, and great man. If He was not what He said He was then I don't want to have anything to do with Him, and I certainly am not going to hold Him up as an example of goodness, and wisdom, and greatness. When one deals with the Christian faith one cannot have one's cake and eat it too!

If you are not a Christian, if you have never encountered Jesus Christ in your life and you believe that most of the Christian faith is pure balderdash, then that is certainly your privilege. However, because I am a Christian and because my views are in such direct contrast to yours one of us is wrong and one of us is right. Why? Because truth is narrow and exclusive.

The Christian faith is like that. Jesus said, "I am the way, and the truth, and the life; no one comes to the Father, but by me" (John 14:6). Either that is a true statement, or it is not a true statement. If it isn't true then a lot of Christians are living a lie and are wasting a lot of time doing it. If it is true, Joe Pagan and Jane Cynic are in trouble. But be that as it may, the point is this: The Christian faith can't be true and not true at the same time.

Second: The truth of the Christian faith is verifiable. This is not a book of Christian apologetics. There are those with ability that far surpasses mine, who can deal adequately with the major themes of that discipline. However, let me make a few comments from personal experience. Most people who feel the Christian faith is intellectually inferior are people who just haven't examined all the data. There was a time in my life when I felt the better educated one became the less one accepted of the Christian faith. That just isn't true unless one's education is either slanted or inferior. Anyone who reads Jean-Paul Sartre, Albert Camus, or Franz Kafka without reading C. S. Lewis should consider his education inferior. Anyone who scoffs at the Christian faith and has not read Pascal, or Aquinas, or Calvin, or Francis Schaeffer and a host of others of like mind, ought to fully understand that his data is insufficient, biased and narrow in its outlook. Anyone who has read Marx and is not just as familiar with the Bible has lost his right to speak with intellectual integrity. It is only a fool or an idiot who stands on the ground of unbelief without any doubts as to the strength of that ground to hold him.

But the truth of the Christian faith is not only verifiable intellectually; it is also verifiable experientially. An honest intellectual search will place the Christian faith in the realm of the believable, but until the unbeliever experiences truth in a personal way he has still not verified the Christian faith. I can talk about the beauty of Cape Cod until you are convinced it is the place to go, but until you have been there you really don't know. It is the same with the Christian faith. There are some things one cannot know until one has tried them; there are truths that are not immediately apparent to the passerby. The ball is over the net with this challenge: take seriously the truth of the Christian faith; try it; experiment with it; and if it doesn't work—if you cannot verify its truth for yourself—then you can become an honest skeptic. Anything less than that and you will never know for sure.

Third: The Christian faith isn't true because it works; works because it is true. If no one ever accepted the claims of Christ, if no one ever took the Christian faith seriously, if no one ever found the meaning and joy that Christ can give to those who follow Him, the Christian faith would still be true. Its truth is something completely separate from the fact that it works. When a person says to me, "Steve, I grew up in the church; I attended Sunday school all my life; I have been a member of the church from age thirteen, and the Christian faith doesn't work," my basic assumption is that the fault is not in the Christian faith but in the person who makes the statement. Why? Because the Christian faith isn't true because it works— it works because it is true. A man who lives in a house with a fully operative shower and plenty of soap does not disprove the power of water and soap because he stays dirty. He proves only his own inability to utilize that which is available to him. It is the same with the Christian faith.

Fourth: The truth of the Christian faith does not come from the genius of man but from the generosity of God. Christianity is a

17

revelation. By that I mean the truth of the Christian faith is that which can only be understood as truth revealed by God to man because God wanted man to know about it. When the Apostle Peter first made his confession that Christ was the Son of God, Jesus said to him, "Blessed are you, Simon Bar-Jona! For flesh and blood has not revealed this to you, but my Father who is in heaven" (Matthew 16:17). In other words Jesus was saying to Peter that what Peter knew about Jesus didn't come from wisdom but from God—it was revealed.

Paul put it this way, "For it is written, 'I will destroy the wisdom of the wise, and the cleverness of the clever I will thwart.' Where is the wise man? Where is the scribe? Where is the debater of this age? Has not God made foolish the wisdom of the world? For since, in the wisdom of God, the world did not know God through wisdom. . . . For Jews demand signs and Greeks seek wisdom, but we preach Christ crucified, a stumbling block to Jews and folly to Gentiles, but to those who are called, both Jews and Greeks, Christ the power of God and the wisdom of God (1 Corinthians 19–21, 22–24). In other words, God is completely other than man. Anything that God wants man to know about Himself God must tell us, otherwise we will not know it.

Fifth: The Christian faith does not contain all truth but it is all true. Someone said to me recently, "Pastor, you are so dogmatic. Don't you believe that truth is to be found anywhere except in the Christian faith?" Of course I do! There is a vast body of truth upon which all men may draw. The Christian faith only claims to have drawn on that truth in questions of faith and life. One of the important things one must understand, for instance, in reading the Bible is that the Bible must dictate the questions it will answer. If you want to find out about Einstein's theory of relativity, don't go to the Bible. If you want to know how to build a school, or make a million dollars, or bake a cake, don't go to the Bible because that isn't the truth about which the Bible speaks. However, if you want to know who you are, what you are doing here, and where you are going, read your Bible. If you want to know the best way to live and die, read your Bible. If you want to know about God, what He is like, what He thinks about you, what

His plans are for you, go to the Bible. All you will find there will be true, but it won't contain all truth.

Sixth: Truth can't be altered to fit circumstances. There are some things about the Christian faith which I don't particularly like (e.g., judgment). If I were the author of the faith I think I would change some things. But, you see, it doesn't matter what I think. Truth is true because it is true. When you are dealing with truth you can't pick and choose that which you like or don't like. You have to accept it because it is truth.

What the Bible has to say about the basic nature of man is not very comforting or acceptable to the modern mind. The Bible says that man is a sinner and separated from God. I don't like that and when I talk to people about God I would like to just skip over it; I would like to just talk about God's love, and His comfort, and His plan for man. Whenever I talk about sin (especially specific sins) I always offend someone. I don't like to offend people, but when one deals with truth, one has no choice but to be truthful. A doctor doesn't refuse to give medicine to a dying man because the medicine tastes bad or because the patient doesn't like needles. A doctor gives medicine because it makes people well. It is the same way with the Christian faith. It could be changed to fit circumstances; it could be softened so as not to offend; it could be compromised so people would accept it. But, you see, if that happened, it wouldn't be the Christian faith and it wouldn't be true.

What I am saying in this chapter is that your faith should never be built on how you feel. It should be built on truth. You should be a Christian and believe the facts of the Christian faith for the same reason you believe two plus two equals four. It's a matter of truth.

2

How to Begin

Jesus answered him "Truly, truly, I say to you, unless one is born anew, he cannot see the kingdom of God."   JOHN 3:3

Therefore, if any one is in Christ, he is a new creation; the old has passed away, behold, the new has come.   2 CORINTHIANS 5:17

"I don't know whether or not I'm a Christian. I think I am, but I'm just not sure." That statement was made to me recently by a young man who only a few years before had given his life to Christ. His fear is not uncommon. Just as there are a lot of people who think they are Christians and who aren't, there are also many Christians who think they aren't or who are not sure about it. The best way to remedy both problems is to find out exactly what it means to be a Christian.

If you should stand before God in the next five minutes and God should say to you, "Can you give Me one reason why I should allow you to come into My kingdom?" what would you say to Him? I have a friend who I am sure would say, "My father was a Presbyterian minister." Some people would say, "I have tried to live a good life; I don't beat my wife and I give my children enough to eat." Others would say, "I have been a member of the church for thirty years! How dare You ask me why I should come into Your kingdom!" There would be many "professional" Christians who would say, "Lord, You must be kidding. I served You all these years. I have preached Your word, and counseled Your people. Why, they even call me Reverend."

The answer God would give all of these admission statements to heaven would be the same answer Jesus talked about in the seventh chapter of Matthew. "On that day many will say to me, 'Lord, Lord, did we not prophesy in your name, and cast out demons in your name, and do many mighty works in your name?' And then will I declare to them, 'I never knew you; depart from me, you evildoers' " (Matthew 7:22, 23).

What then is a Christian? *First:* A Christian is a person who understands that eternal life, abundant life, and new life cannot be earned and are never deserved. They are the free gifts of Christ! Paul put it this way, ". . . the grace of God and the free gift in the grace of that one man Jesus Christ abounded for many" (Romans 5:15). Peter said, "But we believe that we shall be saved through the grace of the Lord Jesus . . ." (Acts 15:11). John said, "For the law was given through Moses; grace and truth came through Jesus Christ" (John 1:17). In Ephesians we read, "For by grace you have been saved through faith; and this is not your own doing, it is the gift of God—not because of works, lest any man should boast" (Ephesians 2:8, 9).

Time after time I have heard people say, "But I can't be a Christian. I'm not good enough." The person who says that or who feels that way just hasn't understood what the Christian faith is all about. New life in Christ is a gift—a free gift. If it were anything else the possibility of our obtaining it would not exist. If a man commits a crime and is sentenced to death, and that man has exhausted all the legal channels for his freedom, the only way he will obtain it is as a free gift from the governor or the president. He can't earn it and, if the courts are right, he doesn't deserve it.

I used to look at some of my friends who seemed to have something I didn't have. They seemed to have a life-style, a joy, a meaning in their lives that I lacked. I noticed they were usually more loving than other people. I observed that they seemed to care about others, that they read their Bible a lot and that they knew how to pray. And so I decided that I would love other people, read the Bible, pray, and smile as much as possible. I even tried teaching in a housing-project

Sunday school. But do you know something? It didn't work. At night when I would take off my smiling mask, when I would have to look in the mirror, when I would have to be honest with myself, I knew that I just didn't make it. No matter how hard I tried I was just not loving. I didn't like reading the Bible, and prayer was a chore. Not only that, after all of the effort and work, I still didn't have what my friends had! You see, nobody told me that what they had was a gift and because it was a gift, it couldn't be earned and it certainly was not deserved.

Second: A Christian is a person who understands the basic nature of man as it applies to himself. Most of us think we and others are fairly decent and good-living. Of course we make some mistakes; of course we sometimes fall into error; of course we don't always quite live up to our goals, but basically we are good people. The Bible says that isn't true. Jeremiah said, "The heart is deceitful above all things, and desperately corrupt; who can understand it?" (Jeremiah 17:9). Paul, the major writer of the New Testament, the first Christian missionary, the man whose work has been reflected in the Church for over nineteen hundred years, and certainly a good man if there ever was a good man said, "I do not understand my own actions. For I do not do what I want, but I do the very thing I hate. For I know that nothing good dwells within me, that is, in my flesh. I can will what is right, but I cannot do it. For I do not do the good I want, but the evil I do not want is what I do" (Romans 7:15, 18, 19).

Perhaps you are saying to yourself, "Now come on, Steve, you aren't still talking about sin. Don't you know that sin went out with my grandfather's spats?" No it didn't! We just thought it did. We aren't any less sinners than we were in your grandfather's time; we just don't talk about it anymore. But lest you disbelieve me, I would refer you to almost every major writer or philosopher of our time. The man who observes people and life, and who writes about it, knows there is a major flaw in human nature—that there is something evil, and corrupt, and wrong at the very heart of things. But lest you still disbelieve me look at yourself. Jesus said, "You, therefore, must be perfect, as your heavenly Father is perfect" (Matthew 5:48). How near do you come to that goal? Are all your thoughts of a nature that it wouldn't bother you if everyone knew them? How about your actions, your secret actions?

You see, most people know they have a problem. It is just that they make a mistake about the type of problem. I have a friend who told me, "Steve, if I could only make another thousand dollars a year, all my problems would be solved." He thought he had a money problem. Some men say, "If I could only get rid of my wife I would have it made. No responsibility, no set hours, no problems." They think they have a wife problem. Some women say, "If I could only get rid of the old grouch, I would have a good life." They think they have a husband problem. There are students who think that everything would be fine if they could only get their education (i.e., a piece of paper with a degree on it). They think they have an education problem. Some people think they have a psychological problem; others think they have a sexual problem, or a drinking problem, or a drug problem. The Bible says all of these people made a mistake in their diagnosis. The Bible says their problem is a sin problem. The Christian understands that fact as it relates to himself.

Third: The Christian understands the great price he must pay for his sin problem. Sin first separates the sinner from others. I see a number of people who have done or said something for which they are ashamed. Often before they will tell me about it they say, "Pastor, what I am about to tell you is in strict confidence. I don't want anyone to know." What they are saying is that they don't want anyone else to know them the way they really are. You see, most of us live behind a mask. We know we aren't good, and pure, and loving, and kind, and honest, and righteous. We just don't want anyone else to know. And so we spend our lives trying to keep our real selves hidden behind the mask. With few exceptions, we allow our sin problem to build a wall between us and the close relationships we ought to have with other people.

Sin not only separates the sinner from others, it separates him from himself. Most people try to run from themselves. As long as they can keep the stereo loud enough, the liquor flowing freely enough and the

24

talk coming fast enough, they don't have to think about the way they really are. The only time we have to face the reality of our sin is at night when we are alone. But mother science has found a way to avoid that too. You take a pill. A sin problem will keep the sinner from facing himself, and being honest, and calling a truce.

But more important than anything else, a sin problem separates the sinner from God. Most of us only think of God as a God of love. That is true but it isn't the whole picture. Not only is God a God of love, He is also a God of justice. In fact, the other side of love is justice. The Bible says, "For the wages of sin is death . . ." (Romans 6:23). Because God is a holy God and man is sinful there is a great chasm between the two. We were created to draw power from God. He is our source, our meaning, our fulfillment. Our problem is that sin keeps us from that source. Just as there is a penalty which must be paid when the law of the land is disobeyed, there is a penalty which must be paid when God's law is broken. That penalty is death. That death isn't just something which comes later either. It is death here and now—spiritual death. You see, there are a lot of dead people still walking around. They just haven't been buried yet.

Fourth: A Christian knows that God has provided only one remedy for our sin problem. Listen to the words of Paul, "While we were yet *helpless,* at the right time Christ died for the *ungodly.* Why, one will hardly die for a righteous man—though perhaps for a good man one will dare even to die. But God shows his love for us in that while we were yet sinners Christ died for us" (Romans 5:6–8). Jesus said, ". . . the Son of man came not to be served but to serve, and to give his life as a ransom for many" (Matthew 20:28). All of man's history points to the hill in the shape of a skull outside the walls of Jerusalem where Jesus died on a cross. His death was not just another good man biting the dust; it was not just the death of a great teacher trying to illustrate a point. On the cross God was a part of man's history in His Son who took upon Himself the sins of the world. He took upon Himself all of that which separates me from others, from myself and from Him. My sin costs me a lot, but it cost God more. It cost Him His Son!

Our position was one which deserved condemnation. In fact, that was the inevitable result. We had been created by God for His purpose and we decided, all of us, to rebel against God and live for ourselves. But Christ paid the penalty; He satisfied the law; He took our place so that we might be free. God took all of my sin—past, present and future—and placed it on His Son. After Jesus died on the cross for my sin, God declared me free. I am now clean and pure in God's sight, not because I am that way in myself, but because Christ was that way for me. Justice has been satisfied. I can now be honest with others and establish close relationships because sin is not the great fact of my life anymore—forgiveness is. I don't have to stay awake at night fighting with my guilt because I'm not guilty anymore. And now, because the great chasm between God and me has been closed with the cross, I can draw upon the power that God offers. As someone has said, "Because of Christ, God took my sin, dumped it in the ocean, and put up a sign which reads: NO FISHING." I don't ever have to be guilty again, or afraid, or lonely, or empty because, "God was in Christ reconciling [Steve Brown] to Himself, not counting [his] trespasses against [him] . . ." (2 Corinthians 5:19).

Finally: The Christian knows that it isn't good enough just to know about grace, and sin and Christ. One must internalize all of that knowledge. In other words, one must individually receive Jesus Christ as Saviour and Lord as an act of the will made in faith. "But to all who *received* him, who *believed* in his name, he gave power to become children of God; who were born, not of blood nor of the will of the flesh nor of the will of man, but of God" (John 1:12–13). Jesus said, "Behold, I stand at the door and knock; if any one hears my voice and opens the door, I will come in to him . . ." (Revelation 3:20).

One time there was a man who was a world renowned tightrope walker. His reputation was known throughout the United States. One of his great publicity stunts was to walk across Niagara Falls on a cable stretched from one end of the falls to the other. On the day he was to perform this great stunt a tremendous crowd assembled to watch. The great artist shouted out to them, "How many of you believe I can walk across those falls." Everyone knew his reputation and most of the people in the crowd shouted, "We know you can!"

26

He did it, and when he had finished he once again shouted out to the crowd, "How many of you believe I can take a wheelbarrow across those falls with a sack of potatoes in it?" The crowd shouted, "We believe you can do it!" He did it, and when he had finished he shouted, "How many of you believe I can take a man across in the wheelbarrow?" Everyone shouted back, "We know you can do it!" The artist pointed to a man standing in the front row and said, "I want you to volunteer." The man turned and all you could see were heels and elbows as he made his way in the opposite direction. You see, he believed with his mind, but he had never internalized that belief.

There are a lot of people just like that man. They believe all of the doctrines but they have never made the step from head knowledge to heart knowledge. If one does not make that step, one does not become a Christian. It's that simple. Jesus promised that if we confess our sins and ask Him to come into our life, He will do just that. When we do it, He then comes to dwell within us and from that point on, no matter what, it is settled.

How do you make that step? You get on your knees and you pray something like this, "Father, I come to You now knowing that I have a terrible sin problem. I don't have anything to offer You; I have nothing which would make me worthy of You. But Jesus died in my place on a cross bearing my sin. I want to accept that gift right now. I want Christ to come into my life right now and take control as my personal Saviour and Lord. From now on I want to live my life for Him. Amen." When we pray that prayer Jesus does exactly what He said He would do. How do I know? I've tried it, and Jesus doesn't lie. One may not feel different, but He promised, and that is enough.

What happens when you become a Christian? *First,* sin is no longer the primary reality in your life. Never again do you have to feel guilty because Jesus took your sin to a cross and set you free. *Second,* you are given eternal life. Eternal life is a gift reserved only for those who have received Christ. He is the only assurance of anything beyond the grave. He said, "I am the resurrection and the life; he who believes in me, though he die, yet shall he live, and whoever lives and believes in me shall never die" (John 11:25, 26). *Third,* you are given a new

27

ability to love others. You can't love until you have been loved and then only to the degree to which you have been loved. When the cross becomes a reality in your life, you have been loved so deeply that it shows in your love for others. *Fourth,* you are given the literal presence of Christ in your life and with that a joy which can come only from Him—a joy not dependent on circumstances. Paul said, "I have been crucified with Christ; it is no longer I who live, but Christ who lives in me . . ." (Galatians 2:20). You never again have to be lonely or without joy! *Finally,* you are no longer on a production basis. Most of us believe that we have to be good enough to please God. If we are good, God will accept us, and if we aren't, He won't. That isn't true after you become a Christian. God not only wipes the slate clean, He throws it away. You belong to the family of God, period. There is nothing you can do which will change the fact of your relationship to Christ. You live a life that grows in grace, and love, and purity, and goodness, and kindness, and understanding not because you have to obtain God's love but because you want to respond to the love you have already received.

When you become a Christian everything doesn't become "sweetness and light." You still sin; you still hurt; you still sometimes feel fear and loneliness. But now you have a way out. Now you have a Father whose power is without limit. Before you weren't even in His family. That is why the Christian faith is such good news. If that good news has been internalized in your life once, you don't have to do it again. If you have given your life to Christ don't let anyone tell you that you don't belong to Christ. It's a lie and it ought to be treated as you would treat any lie. If you have never made the step into the family of God, do it now. Everything depends on that step—everything!

What would I say to God if I should face Him in the next five minutes and He should ask me, "Can you give Me one reason why I should allow you to come into My kingdom?" I would say to God, my Father, "Lord, I haven't done anything deserving of Your acceptance of me. But Jesus died on the cross for my sin. You promised that if I confessed my sin and received Jesus as my Saviour, I would be justified in Your sight. You don't lie. That is the only ground on which I have to stand." That would be enough.

If you have been a Christian before, I hope this chapter has given you some help as a review of how you began your new life and as assurance that you have received it. If you received Christ for the first time after reading this chapter, Happy Birthday!

3
How to Live in the Stream of Power

But you shall receive power when the Holy Spirit has come upon you. . . .   ACTS 1:8

I am writing this while listening to the radio broadcast of a baseball game between the Boston Red Sox and the Chicago White Sox. At this particular stage of the season the Red Sox aren't doing too well. One of the reasons for this is the poor showing of Luis Aparicio, the Red Sox shortstop. He is a great fielder, and this season has shown it. But Aparicio is also a great hitter and so far this season he has gone some thirty games without a hit. To the dismay of the Red Sox fans, Aparicio is now in the longest hitting slump of his career. There are a lot of Christians who live the life of faith the same way Luis Aparicio is playing baseball right now. They are certainly in the game, but the power is gone. What do you do when the power is gone? Let's talk about it.

First, let's examine the promises. Jesus promised that those who follow Him will have abundant life: "I came that they may have life, and have it abundantly" (John 10:10). He said that there would be joy and peace: "These things I have spoken to you, that my joy may be in you, and that your joy may be full" (John 15:11). "Peace I leave with you; my peace I give to you; not as the world gives do I give to you" (John 14:27). Jesus gives meaning: "I am the way, and the truth, and the life . . ." (John 14:6). Jesus promised that many of the great works He performed would be performed by Christians: "Truly, truly, I say to you, he who believes in me will also do the works that I do;

and greater works than these will he do, because I go to the Father" (John 14:12). Jesus promised that we could have power when we witnessed to others about Him: "But you shall receive power when the Holy Spirit has come upon you; and you shall be my witnesses in Jerusalem and in all Judea and Samaria and to the end of the earth" (Acts 1:8). Jesus promised that we would have prayer power: "And whatever you ask in prayer, you will receive, if you have faith" (Matthew 21:22). The Bible teaches that the Christian can have power to resist temptation: "No temptation has overtaken you that is not common to man. God is faithful, and he will not let you be tempted beyond your strength, but with the temptation will also provide the way of escape, that you may be able to endure it" (1 Corinthians 10:13). God promises in the Bible that Christians will live a life that bears the fruit of the Spirit: "But the fruit of the Spirit is love, joy, peace, patience, kindness, goodness, faithfulness, gentleness, self-control . . ." (Galatians 5:22, 23).

Now let me ask you a question. Be honest with yourself because no one will know how you answer except you. Using the above criteria as the measurement, does your faith work? If your toaster doesn't make toast you either get it fixed or you get a new one. If you can't get your hair spray to hold you try another brand. If your automobile breaks down you either get it fixed or you get another one. It should be the same way with your faith. One time a missionary who ran a mission school was asked by one of his pupils, "Father, do you really believe that God is our Father." "Of course I do," replied the missionary. "Then," said the little boy, "Why do you worry so much?" Perhaps a lot of our friends wonder about us too.

A man once approached Dwight L. Moody. "Mr. Moody," he said, "you probably don't even think I am a Christian." Moody replied, "Not a red-hot one." One of the problems in the modern day church is not so much that there aren't Christians, but that there aren't very many red-hot ones. This is not a new problem. Paul faced it in the early church at Corinth. Listen to what he says, "But I, brethren, could not address you as spiritual men, but as men of the flesh [carnal men], as babes in Christ, I fed you with milk, not solid food; for you were not ready for it; and even yet you are not ready, for you are still of the flesh" (1 Corinthians 3:1–3). In other words, Paul is saying that there are three kinds of people in the world: the non-Christian, the carnal Christian and the spiritual Christian. The first needs no detailed explanation. The non-Christian is the person who has decided to have nothing to do with Christ; he has decided that he can make it on his own. Let's look in more detail at the last two, the carnal Christian and the spiritual Christian.

When a person first receives Christ as Saviour and Lord there are a number of different responses which can follow. Some Christians "grab the ball and run with it." These Christians find everything new; they are radiant and alive; they live the life of faith in such a way as to give evidence of the grace that is working in them. Others receive Christ and immediately begin to doubt their experience. They waver and vacillate until their lives are no different than before they met Christ. But by far the greatest number of new Christians come into the church and wither away on some committee (a group of the unwilling, appointed by the incompetent, to do the unnecessary). They develop "churchitis," a disease which affects the spiritual nerve tissue and destroys the power cells. And then they become frustrated, empty, unfruitful Christians. As Sam Shoemaker put it, they never go far enough for the fun.

The question before us is this: How does a carnal Christian become a spiritual Christian with all of the side benefits that it entails? The Christian faith is not so much a way to live as it is a place to live— in a stream of power. How does one get into that stream of power? A friend of mine once said, "Steve, I feel sometimes that I am living on the outside of a balloon filled with power. Sometimes, if I am lucky, I can stick a pin in and receive just a little. I only wish I could live in the center of the balloon." How does one live in the center of power?

The Bible teaches that the source of power in the Christian life is the Holy Spirit, the third person of the Trinity. The Holy Spirit is portrayed in art with the symbol of fire. That is no accident. Fire is the appropriate symbol for what the Christian life ought to be—alive, consuming, exciting, revolutionary. The commandment of Scripture to the Christian is that the Christian ought to "be filled [i.e., controlled and empowered] with the Spirit" (Ephesians 5:18). But this filling of the Holy Spirit is not only a command, it is also a promise, "But you shall receive power when the Holy Spirit has come upon you . . ." (Acts 1:8). In other words the heritage of the Christian is the fulfilled life as given by the Holy Spirit. With anything less than that the Christian has missed the point, and has not claimed his heritage. If you are living the life of frustration, and defeat, and emptiness, if you have a bad case of the "spiritual blahs," you didn't get those things from Christ! He doesn't sell things like that in His store.

Our problem: a lack of power. Our text: ". . . be filled with the Spirit" (Ephesians 5:18). The question is, how do you become filled (i.e., controlled and empowered) by the Holy Spirit? Let me give you six principles that every Christian ought to know. *One:* Being filled with the Holy Spirit is not a request on the part of God. It is a commandment! The reason God wants His children to be filled with the Holy Spirit is very simple. The Christian life is not difficult—*it is impossible.* No one can live the way Christ wants us to live or with the abundance about which He spoke, by himself. It is impossible. That is why God has provided gasoline for the engine. That gasoline is the Holy Spirit. You can have an engine so big and powerful that you will be able to pass every vehicle on the road. But if you don't have gasoline in the engine, you will only be able to stand and admire your new automobile. It is the same with the Christian faith. Without the Holy Spirit, nothing happens.

Two: God never commands us to do anything for which He does not provide the means to do it. When God told Moses to go and bring the Hebrew people out of Egypt, Moses didn't think he could do it. In fact, he was not equipped for such a task. He couldn't speak properly and even if he could, the Pharaoh would not listen. But God provided a spokesman in Aaron and the power for Moses to perform miracles so the Pharaoh would listen. "But Moses said to the Lord, 'Oh, my Lord, I am not eloquent, either heretofore or since thou hast spoken to thy servant; but I am slow of speech and of tongue. . . . Then the Lord said to him, '. . . Is there not Aaron, your brother, the Levite? I know that he can speak well. . . . Go back to Egypt; . . . see that you do before Pharaoh all the miracles which I have put in your power . . ." (Exodus 4:10, 14, 21). When God asks you to do anything He does not leave you without the means to do that which He has asked. *Three:* As children of God we are allowed to ask and receive anything which is within the will of God. "And this is the confidence which we have in him, that if we ask anything according to his will he hears us. And if we know that he hears us in whatever we ask, we know that we have obtained the request made of him" (1 John 5:14, 15). If I ask God to destroy my enemy, I can be sure he won't do it. Why? Because that would probably not be in the will of God. The same goes for my asking God to give me a million dollars or to grant me sunshine for my golf game. However, when I ask anything which is in God's will, the Bible promises that He not only hears, but that He also answers in the affirmative. Our being filled with the Holy Spirit is in God's will because He told us so. There is no question about the propriety of asking God for the filling of the Spirit unless He lied to us in the first place, and He didn't.

Four: Just as sin keeps us from salvation, so sin keeps us from obtaining the power of the Holy Spirit. I quoted to you before from 1 Corinthians, the third chapter. Let me give you the whole quote: "But I, brethren, could not address you as spiritual men, but as men of the flesh, as babes in Christ. I fed you with milk, not solid food; for you were not ready for it; and even yet you are not ready, for you are still of the flesh. For while there is jealousy and strife among you, are you not of the flesh, and behaving like ordinary men?" (1 Corinthians 3:1–3). In other words that which prevented the people of Corinth from becoming spiritual Christians was their jealousy and their strife (i.e., their sin).

There are two positions of the Christian. One is the Christian's relationship to God, and the other is the Christian's fellowship with God. You come into relationship to God when you believe on the name of Christ (John 1:12). That relationship is established. At the time you become a Christian you become a literal child of God. Just as your earthly father doesn't kick you out of the house or disown you for infractions of his rules (unless you have a particularly unloving father), God doesn't disown us for infractions of His rules. However, there is a penalty to be paid. Our sin, while it doesn't destroy our relationship with God, does destroy our fellowship with Him. Sin, no matter how small or insignificant, becomes a blockage in God's channel of power. When there is unconfessed sin, we are cut off from our source of power which is the Holy Spirit. The most miserable person in the world isn't the person who has never received Christ. The most miserable person in the world is the Christian who is out of fellowship with God.

Five: In order for the Christian to be a spiritual Christian and be filled with the Holy Spirit, that Christian must either never sin (which is difficult unless you are dead) or remove his sin by confession (which is always possible for the Christian). Listen to God's promise: "If we confess our sins [the ones we know about], he is faithful and just, and will forgive our sins and cleanse us from all unrighteousness [the sins of which we aren't aware]" (1 John 1:9).

There is absolutely no excuse for a Christian going around with a guilt complex. That is an affront to the cross of Christ! You, as a Christian, have been provided a way to completely remove guilt as a factor in your life. God sent His Son to do that for you. All you have to do is appropriate it for yourself according to the promise in 1 John 1:9. If you don't, it is your own fault and you should not receive anybody's sympathy.

Six: Just as you received Christ for salvation by faith, you must receive the Holy Spirit by faith. If you are really serious about getting serious with God, if you really want to be controlled and empowered by the Holy Spirit, get on your knees and pray a prayer similar to this: "Father, I come before You confessing the fact that I have controlled my own life and that I have made a mess out of it. I want You, in the Holy Spirit, to once again come in and take control absolutely and completely. You have commanded that I be filled with the Holy Spirit (Ephesians 5:18). I accept that command. Right now I confess before You my sin (1 John 1:9) and claim Your promise that if I ask in faith You will respond in fact (1 John 5:14, 15). Because You do not lie, I thank You for coming into my life and filling me with Your Spirit. Amen."

That is the kind of prayer that must usually be prayed many times. Each time we sin and are convicted about that sin, we ought to agree

36

with God that it is sin, confess it, and once again ask Him to take control of our lives. One of the most amazing things Jesus ever said is this, "I am the vine, you are the branches. He who abides in me, and I in him, he it is that bears much fruit, for apart from me you can do nothing" (John 15:5). Jesus is talking about being filled with the Holy Spirit, about being so connected to Him that you will act only in obedience to Him. Without that, there is nothing.

Now let's see how these principles work themselves out in actual life. Let's assume that you have an anger problem. Let's assume further that the problem is related especially to one person. Whenever you see that person you find yourself becoming angry. Then because you can't deal with the problem you find that you are feeling guilty, that you are having trouble praying and that you are out of fellowship with God. What do you do? You utilize the principles about which we have been talking. You pray, "Father, You know this problem and You know my anger. You know how much trouble I am having loving that old so-and-so. This is a sin and it is interfering with my life with You. I now confess before You my sin. I confess that I am in control of my life. I ask Your Spirit to once again take control and through me to love and understand and care for this person. I thank You for doing through me what I can't do by myself. Amen."

When that prayer is prayed sincerely, the Holy Spirit begins once again to take control. It may take a while (especially if the old so-and-so is a real pill) but it will work, and you will discover a new way to live—controlled and empowered by the Holy Spirit.

Now, isn't that better than the spiritual blahs?

4

How to Use the Bible

All scripture is inspired by God and profitable for teaching, for reproof, for correction, and for training in righteousness, that the man of God may be complete, equipped for every good work. TIMOTHY 3:16, 17

In his book, *Journey Into Light,* Emile Cailliet reports on his first encounter with the Bible. Before discovering the Bible, his philosophical naturalism had prevented him from presupposing God as necessary for anything. He said that he had tried to find a book that understood him, and had finally decided to compile one for himself. But as he read through the book he had compiled he knew the futility of his efforts. His wife at that time presented him with a Bible. He had never seen one before but, in his own words, "I literally grabbed the book and rushed to my study with it. I opened it and chanced upon the beatitudes! I read, and read, and read—now aloud with an indescribable warmth surging within . . . I could not find words to express my awe and wonder. And suddenly the realization dawned upon me: This was the Book that would understand me! I needed it so much, yet, unaware, I had attempted to write my own—in vain. I continued to read deeply into the night, mostly from the gospels. And lo and behold, as I looked through them, the One of whom they spoke, the One who spoke and acted in them, became alive to me. . . . A decisive insight flashed through my whole being the following morning as I probed the opening chapters of the Gospel according to John. The very clue to the secret of human life was disclosed right there, not stated in the foreboding language of philosophy but in the common, everyday language of human circumstances."

It may suprise you to know that I had been a Christian a long time before I began to take the Bible seriously. I realized my sin problem; I knew that God's only remedy for my sin problem was the cross of Christ; I had accepted Christ as my Saviour and Lord, but, for a long time, I thought one would have to sacrifice intellectual integrity in order to accept the Bible as God's written Word. I took some Bible courses in college which tended to sustain my warped view of intellectual integrity, and my seminary training did nothing to change that view (in fact, it warped it further). I had somewhere been conned into the idea that anyone who really believed the Bible to be God's Word must either be an unthinking fundamentalist or a fool. You see, I was one of the educated. That meant, among other things, that one must bow in the direction of the Bible. (It certainly was a great work of literature, it certainly had had a tremendous influence on mankind, it certainly "contained" truth.) But as far as really believing it, and acting on its words, that was for the masses, not for us educated types.

And then one day I stopped running for a moment and it dawned on me that something was missing. The God who had seemed so real to me before seemed so far away and irrelevant now. The faith that had come into my life when I first met Christ was no longer real or alive. The promise I had made when I gave my life to Christ seemed now in retrospect to be no more than a whimsy. A friend of mine (who incidentally was a professor at a very fine Christian college) diagnosed my problem. He said that I was lost because I didn't have a map, and that the map of the Christian was the Bible.

At the time I smiled at my friend in my educated, arrogant way, and thought to myself, "He's honest, but he's wrong." However, I did agree to read some books he had suggested to me, and to try to give the Bible a chance to speak on its own. Both suggestions proved invaluable. The first suggestion allowed me to see, for the first time in my life, that one did not have to sacrifice one whit of intellectual integrity to believe in the Bible, any more than a scientist had to sacrifice intellectual integrity when he accepted the law of gravity. The first suggestion allowed me to see that my view of unthinking fundamentalists was unthinking, that scholars in many fields were "men of the Book" and didn't mind saying so.

The second suggestion my friend gave me opened a whole new world. For once I opened the Bible without a book about the Bible open beside it. For once I told Graf, and Wellhausen, and Dibelius, and Bultmann to stand aside for a while so I could look for myself. What I found was exciting. With Cailliet, I found a book that understood me; I found ultimate answers to ultimate questions; I found an outline of God's plan for history; I found the plan God had for my own life; I found a source of authority; I found a world view that made sense. But most of all I found in the Bible a God who speaks, and acts, and cares. When I open the Bible now, it is not to read a great piece of literature, nor to find a proof text for my pet theological system, nor to find something to quote for my more conservative parishioners. When I open the Bible now, it is to listen to God speaking, to get, as it were, some fresh word from the Lord.

Now, having given testimony to what I know to be true, let me give you some basic presuppositions and then some basic principles that every Christian ought to know. The *first* presupposition is this: *God isn't in the business of confusing His people.* A lot of people think that God shrouds His will for us in mystery and then enjoys watching us spend the rest of our lives trying to solve the mystery. That just isn't so. God wants us to spend our lives living, not searching for how He wants us to live. If God exists and wants to communicate something to His creatures (which I consider axiomatic) then He will do exactly that, in a way which is clear and understandable.

The *second* presupposition is this: *God's will is something too important to be entrusted to the emotional whimsy of a fad-conscious humanity.* I once worked in a radio station which was owned by a man who was a nut about memos. If I wanted to say hello to him when I came to the station, I almost had to put it down on a memo. No matter what directive came from anyone to anyone it had to be in the form of a memo. This man's wife worked at the station with him, and I often wondered if he sent her a memo before they went to bed to tell her good-night. But, do you know something? As much as I hated those memos, I found that he had a point. There is so much confusion

41

when directions are given by word of mouth, so much misunderstanding, so many mistakes, that it is always better to write it down. That, I suppose, was in the mind of God when, in His infinite wisdom, He decided to write it down.

The *third* presupposition is this: *The Bible is the only infallible rule of faith and practice,—all of it!* I have to assume, before I read the Bible (because I know my own limitations) that the Bible is the authority; my decision about it is not. The Bible teaches about heaven and hell. I like the former and I don't like the latter. If I accept the former and refuse to accept the latter as true, then I am picking truth and using myself as the authority for truth. However, if I want to really know truth I have to trust the source (i.e., the Bible) for that truth, not my judgment of it. It is arrogant to assume that I have the wisdom, when I read the Bible, to determine what is true and what isn't. If some of it is true, then all of it is; if some of it is not true, then there is a very good possibility that none of it is.

And the *final* presupposition: *Christianity without a belief in the Bible as God's written Word, is not Christianity.* Jesus used the Bible (the Old Testament) as His authority. He quoted from it (Matthew 4:4, 7, 10; 12:3; Mark 10:2, 3, etc.); He based His argumentation on a single expression of a text (Matthew 22:32; 43–45); and, He assumed the importance of all of it (Luke 16:17; Luke 18:32). Just a cursory reading of the New Testament will show that the apostles held the same view of Scripture which was held by Jesus. When one considers the great personages in the history of the Church who have held to a belief in the authority and trustworthiness of the Bible, it becomes a roll call of the saints—Clement of Alexandria, Gregory of Nazianzus, Augustine, John Chrysostom, Athanasius, Origen, Jerome, Irenaeus, Aquinas, Luther, Calvin, Wesley, Carey, Whitfield, Edwards, Moody, Morgan, Spurgeon and many, many more. Every major creed of the Christian church from its inception has either assumed a belief in the authority of Scripture or has stated it. It is difficult for me to see how any theological system without the Bible as God's written Word, could be called Christian.

Now let's turn to the main consideration of this chapter: How does one use the Bible? As I read the Bible I apply five principles which

I believe to be basic for the Christian who has decided to take the Bible seriously. *First:* When you read the Bible you should read it in the knowledge that God is speaking to you and that His Spirit will make it real and apply it. Listen to what Jesus said, "I have yet many things to say to you, but you cannot bear them now. When the Spirit of truth comes, he will guide you into all the truth; for he will not speak on his own authority, but whatever he hears he will speak, and he will declare to you the things that are to come" (John 16:12, 13). In these words we have the real key to understanding the Bible. If you approach the Bible with the attitude that with your superior knowledge and wisdom you will discern the mind of God, you will go away empty. However, if you approach the Bible with a prayer for God's Spirit to guide you, you will find riches you never dreamed possible.

Second: A Christian ought to read the Bible with some measure of intelligence. Now I'm not talking about your educational background, or your knowledge of hermeneutical principles, or your familiarity with Biblical theology and scholarship. I am talking about the use of your mind under the guidance of the Holy Spirit. Jesus was once asked about the greatest commandment and He answered, "The first is, 'Hear, O Israel: The Lord our God, the Lord is one; and you shall love the Lord your God with all your heart, and with all your soul, and *with all your mind,* and with all your strength'" (Mark 12:29, 30). Jesus understood that the mind was not something one discards when thinking thoughts of God; He knew that the mind of man, when given over to God's Spirit, is a tool used by God to bring forth righteous knowledge. He knew that intelligence and commitment are not mutually exclusive—so should we.

You see, the Bible has been used to support everything from the flatness of the earth to the superiority of the white race. It has been dragged out to do service at the bidding of capitalism and socialism. It has been used to proof text everything from child sacrifice to the death of God. Don't ever fall into the trap of using one verse to support any view. Don't ever use the Bible to support your views— allow your views to be molded by the Bible. That is the purpose of using the Bible intelligently.

Third: When you read the Bible, use the proper principles of inter-

43

pretation. Get a good commentary or study Bible. Before you read a book of the Bible, find out why it was written and to whom it was written. Try to discover the date, the authorship, and the background of the book. Place the book in its proper perspective. Understand that the language of the Bible is primarily phenomenal (i.e., the language of appearance) rather than scientific. When the Bible speaks of the sun rising and setting it is describing an appearance, not giving a scientific analysis. Understand the progressive nature of revelation. The New Testament interprets the Old Testament; the letters interpret the Gospels; the whole Bible interprets its parts. And when you don't understand a text, or chapter or verse, don't just skip over it. Study it; see what others have said about it; ponder it until you have it.

Fourth: Be regular and systematic in your Bible study. Too many Christians practice Biblical smorgasbord—they read the Bible at the place where it falls open, or they read those portions they like or with which they are familiar. A woman told me recently in response to my asking her if she had a daily encounter with the Bible, that she read the twenty-third Psalm every day. Now I like the twenty-third Psalm too, but if the twenty-third Psalm is the extent of my Biblical knowledge I am to be pitied. The Bible is not an easy book to read. If anyone has ever told you that it is, don't believe them. Some portions are easier than others, but as a whole, the Bible will yield itself only to a concerted effort and regular Bible study. Being familiar with the Bible is a lifelong process and it will take all you can give it.

It is best to choose a book for study, and then to find out everything you can about that particular book. Then each day read a portion of that book. Don't see how fast you can get through it. Read only as much as you can understand and absorb. (For some it is only a few verses and for others it is one or two chapters.) When you finish your study go back over the book, and check yourself on what you have learned. God honors regular and systematic Bible study and, no matter what you have heard about people who open the Bible at random and find guidance, far more people find God speaking to them in systematic Bible study than with the hit-or-miss method.

Finally: Don't just acquire knowledge about the Bible; don't just add to your list of Biblical doctrines; don't just become familar with what the Bible says. Apply that which you read to yourself and to your life situations. Whenever you read the Bible, ask yourself: What does this have to say to me? What have I learned which will make a difference in my life? What has God told me to do? Let me illustrate what I mean. When I read the thirteenth chapter of 1 Corinthians, it should be read like this:

If Stephen Brown speaks in the tongues of men and of angels, but has not love, he is a noisy gong or a clanging cymbal. And if Stephen has prophetic powers, and understands all mysteries and all knowledge, and if Stephen has all faith, so as to remove mountains, but has not love, he is nothing. If Stephen gives away all that he has, and if he delivers his body to be burned, but has not love, Stephen Brown will gain nothing. The love that Stephen ought to have should make him patient and kind; it should keep him from being jealous or boastful; it should not make him arrogant or rude. The love that ought to control Stephen would keep him from insisting on his own way; it would keep him from being irritable or resentful; it would prevent him from rejoicing at wrong, but would enable him to rejoice in the right. The love that Stephen ought to have would cause him to bear all things, to believe all things, to hope for all things and to endure all things. That kind of love will never end; if Stephen speaks a prophecy, it will pass away; if Stephen speaks in a tongue, it will cease; if Stephen acquires great knowledge, it will pass away. For Stephen's knowledge is imperfect, and his prophecy is imperfect; but when the perfect comes, the imperfect will pass away. When Stephen was a child, he spoke like a child, he thought like a child, he reasoned like a child; when he became a man, he gave up childish ways. For now Stephen sees in a mirror dimly, but then he will see face to face. Now Stephen knows in part; then he will understand fully, even as he has been fully understood. So faith, hope, love abide, these three; but the greatest possession Stephen could have is love.

45

One of the finest privileges the Christian has is his study of the Bible. Its riches will sustain, and guide, and undergird, and comfort. Its words will be unto him, God's words. Its doctrines will make truth clear and communicable. The life of which it speaks will change society and make all things new.

An American businessman once came upon a native in Africa who was studying his Bible. With that kind of impudence which has created the image of the Ugly American he said, "In my country, that book is old-fashioned and out-of-date." The African scarcely looking up from his Bible, and with a smile said, "If that book were out-of-date here, you would have been eaten by now."

5

How to Have a Meaningful Prayer Life

*And when they had prayed, the place in which they were gathered
together was shaken. . . .*   ACTS 4:31

"And when they had prayed, the place in which they were
gathered together was shaken . . ." (Acts 4:31). Tell that to Joe
Pagan and see what he says. He will tell you that it didn't happen, or if it did, it was just a coincidence that it happened after
they had prayed. Tell it to most church members and they will
tell you that things were different in those days. Think about it
yourself, and you will probably wonder why places don't shake
anymore when Christians pray.

Listen to what Jesus said about prayer: "Whatever you ask in my
name, I will do it, that the Father may be glorified in the Son; if you
ask anything in my name, I will do it" (John 14:13, 14). That is a
pretty fantastic statement! If it is a true statement then the most
awesome power in the world is prayer power. If it is true, then a lot
of churches and a lot of Christians are doing something wrong. It is
the presupposition of this chapter that Jesus knew what He was
talking about, that He was making a statement of fact when He said
that prayer could bring tremendous results.

I have observed, however, that most people aren't so interested in
tremendous results. Most people really don't care whether or not they
move mountains or whether or not they raise the dead or heal the sick.
They would be satisfied if only they knew that God hears their pray-

ers, that He cares, that He is touched with their hurt. A woman said, "When I pray, I feel so empty and silly. If only I knew that Someone heard my words or even cared that I was speaking, I could face anything." Her need is universal! All men have a deep abiding need that Someone will listen to their hurt—and care.

Our questions are these: What causes places to shake when Christians pray? How does one communicate in a meaningful way with God? How does one go about praying in such a way so as to be heard? The Christian who doesn't understand the Biblical doctrine of prayer is like Carl Yastrzemski without a baseball bat. He has the possibility of power, but he doesn't have the tools to make the possibility a reality. Let's talk about those tools.

The first tool is relationship. The Christian faith, stripped of all but the most essential, is a relationship to a Person. Within and because of that relationship there is the possibility of communion and fellowship. Without the relationship there is the superficial small talk one always finds between strangers. If you have received Christ into your life, if you have encountered Him in your darkness and received His light, you are now in a position to communicate. If your prayer life is empty and frustrating the first thing you ought to do is to check that relationship (chapter 2). If the relationship is there then, secondly, you ought to check whether or not the relationship is a speaking relationship (chapter 3). A man who had been through a terrible crisis said that he had prayed to God and God didn't answer his prayer. "Therefore," he said, "I will never pray again." I asked him if, when he went to God he knew the God to whom he was speaking. He thought about that, and it dawned on him that his problem had been a problem of relationship. The next time he prayed it was to establish a relationship. That relationship changed his life, and from that changed life there flowed prayer which was real and effective.

The second tool is faith. Listen to what Jesus said about faith: "Have faith in God. Truly, I say to you, whoever says to this mountain, 'Be taken up and cast into the sea,' and does not doubt in his heart, but believes that what he says will come to pass, it will be done for him. Therefore I tell you, whatever you ask in prayer, believe that you receive it, and you will" (Mark 11:22–24). In other words, Jesus was saying that if we really believe, anything is possible.

Now here is the catch. Faith isn't something you can turn off and on at will; it isn't something that you can just say you are going to have and have. The kind of faith about which Jesus was speaking is not easy and requires a lifetime of growth. When you were a baby you didn't start running the first day out of the crib. First, you learned to crawl, and then you learned to walk, and then you learned to run. Faith is the same kind of process. It takes a while. Those people who can pray big prayers believing that God will intervene, and then who see God doing exactly that, are people who have first learned to crawl by asking for small things. Someone tells of a woman who had a gigantic mountain behind her house which blocked the view. She read how Jesus had promised that if we prayed properly we could see mountains moved. And so she prayed for God to remove the mountain. The next morning she opened the curtains, looked out, and said, "Just as I thought; it is still there." The fact is that there aren't many of us who have enough faith to see a mountain "moved into the sea." If we don't have that kind of faith, it is useless to ask. Better to start with small things.

In my church there is a group of young women who meet once a week for prayer. Most of these women were not mature, experienced Christians. But they were determined to learn something about the Bible and to learn something about prayer. They promised each other that each person would pray for the others in the group by name each day. Also, they began to build a corporate prayer list which each used every day. At first nothing happened, but after only a few short weeks God began answering some of their little prayers. Every time God answered a prayer their faith grew stronger, and God, in response to that faith, answered more and more of their prayers. Now it is suprising how many people call these women to ask for prayer. (If they were to pray for the

49

ceiling to fall, I am sure I would crawl under a chair.)

That is a good example of how faith grows. You may not have the faith to ask God to use you to change the world, but everyone has enough faith to ask God to help him be effective in the life of just one other person. When God answers that prayer (and He will) you will find your faith in the power of God has grown. That kind of faith has a mushrooming effect, and by it great men of prayer are made.

The third tool is fellowship. It is interesting to note that the Lord's Prayer is a corporate prayer (e.g., *Our* Father. . . . Give *us* this day *our* daily bread. . . . Forgive *us our* debts. . . . etc.). Jesus was trying to tell us something. He said, "For where two or three are gathered in my name, there am I in the midst of them" (Matthew 18:20). The women in that prayer group had not only learned the need of faith, they had learned the need of fellowship. If you aren't praying regularly with someone else, you ought to. It will bind you together, but it will also bind you to God. His promise of presence is clear if we will only accept it.

The fourth tool is forgiveness—of others. Jesus said, "And whenever you stand praying, forgive, if you have anything against any one; so that your Father also who is in heaven may forgive you your trespasses" (Mark 11:25). Time and time again Jesus emphasized the importance of forgiveness as the prerequisite for effective prayer. A friend of mine who held a terrible grudge against another man finally was able to overcome his bitterness and forgive. My friend went to this man and said, "Bill, I forgive you—now I can pray again!" If you think your prayers are being stopped by the ceiling, if you feel frustrated after you pray, think about those people you haven't forgiven. That may be the reason.

The fifth tool is regularity in prayer. Some people pray the way they go to church—twice a year. And then when they do pray they can't understand why they don't get through. Now I want you to notice that I'm not telling you to pray long prayers (the way for a new Christian to quickly become discouraged is to set aside an hour a day for prayer and then find difficulty in praying for two minutes). The point is that your prayers should be regular. The problem with a lot of Christians is that they pray when they feel like praying. If they are feeling especially spiritual on any given day, then they pray. If they don't feel spiritual then they don't pray. Don't ever let your feelings interfere with your regular practice of prayer. How you feel has nothing to do with how God listens. Every day, set aside a specific time for prayer; don't allow anything to interfere with that time except a funeral—yours.

The final and perhaps the most important tool is obedience. When you go to prayer you ought to be aware that if prayer doesn't change you, it won't change anything else. The reason Christ could make as fantastic a statement as, "Whatever you ask in my name, I will do it . . ." (John 14:13) is because He understood that when a person learns enough about prayer to enable that person to ask for anything and get it, that person doesn't want anything outside the will of God. Prayer is a time when we pour out our hurts and needs to God, but it is much more than that. It is a time when we submit ourselves to Him for His judgment and disposition on those needs and hurts. Prayer is a time when we go to God without any reservations about doing what He says to do. The prayer which brings results is this: "Father, I have come now before You asking that You show me Your will, that You give me Your plan for my life, that You mold me into Your image. . . ." The heavens are open for that kind of prayer! Why do you think God honored the prayers of Wesley for England and the prayers of Whitfield for America? I'll tell you why: because their prayers were not mere exercises in getting God to do what they wanted Him to do. Their prayers were exercises in obedience. Prayer is always a two-way conversation between you and God. You certainly speak to God, but you must also listen (in the Scripture, in the "still small voice," in the circumstances of your life) in order to be conformed to His will for you.

Now, assuming you have understood and appropriated the proper tools and you want to pray, how do you pray? What exactly do you say? How do you go about really praying? Jesus answered those questions in the Sermon on the Mount and His answer was the Lord's Prayer:

> Our Father who art in heaven,
> Hallowed be thy name.
> Thy kingdom come,
> Thy will be done,
>> On earth as it is in heaven.
> Give us this day our daily bread;
> And forgive us our debts,
>> As we also have forgiven our debtors;
> And lead us not into temptation
>> But deliver us from evil.

MATTHEW 6:9–13

In this prayer Jesus was not just giving us a formal prayer He wanted us to pray in our worship services; He was also giving us the basic elements in prayer. Let's look at the content of His prayer. First, Jesus allows us to see how we can approach God once we become a Christian. The Bible says that once we receive Christ, once we believe in and trust in Him, we become His child (John 1:12). We can now talk to God as a child talks to his father. You don't have to be formal with a loving father; you don't have to hedge and play games when you are talking to a loving father; you don't have to pick and choose the right words when you are speaking to a loving father. You see, a father like that is approached in the knowledge that he wants to hear what you say, no matter how you say it, no matter how perfect the English, no matter how well balanced the phrases. Jesus said God is like that. You may talk to Him the way you would talk to a loving father. Jesus said to pray, "Our Father. . . ."

However, Jesus also wanted to make clear that one does not become flippant with God. He added, ". . . who art in heaven. . . ." And then at the end of the prayer He added, to emphasize our position of

52

weakness and finiteness, "And lead us not into temptation, but deliver us from evil [or the evil one]." God, although our Father, is still God. He ought to be approached with the understanding that our position is always one of weakness, and need and finitude. He is an omnipotent Father, not "that big fellow in the sky," or "the man upstairs," or, as one movie star put it, "a living doll." Address God as Father, but remember that your Father is God.

Then, in the Lord's Prayer, Jesus gives us the three elements that ought to be in every prayer, a checklist that will form the outline of the Christian's prayer. *First,* there is praise. Jesus said to pray, ". . . Hallowed be Thy name." Whenever you pray you ought to specifically set aside a portion of that prayer for praise. You are very fortunate to have the privilege of praying to God—tell Him so. You have seen God act in your life and you ought to be very grateful—tell Him so. You have been given life with all of the blessings that go with life and you ought to be thankful to God—tell Him so. You have been given difficult circumstances, and hurt, and pain, to make you strong, and you ought to be grateful to God—tell Him so. God is everything; He is love, and truth, and life; *He is God*—tell Him so. A good rule of thumb is to always praise God more than you petition God. Make praise central to your prayer life.

Second, confession is important. Jesus said to pray, "And forgive us our debts, as we forgive our debtors. . . ." If you read the third chapter of this book you are aware that the Bible teaches that sin keeps Joe Pagan from salvation, but it also keeps Joe Christian from fellowship. Unconfessed sin in your life will hurt your communication with God. The spiritual power that enables you to live your life in Christ, and even makes your prayer life meaningful, is blocked off by your sin. Confess your sin to God (1 John 1:9) and determine, by His grace, to turn from it, and the power that comes from God will once again fill you up and make you clean. When I have difficulty praying, more often than not, it is because there is unconfessed sin in my life. That could be your problem too.

Finally, a portion of our prayer should be given over to petition,

Jesus said, to pray, "Give us this day our daily bread. . . ." God is concerned with every aspect of your life; He knows your name; He cares when you are afraid and lonely; He is attentive to your needs. If you have anything in your life that is big enough to bother you, it is also big enough to bother God. There are two extremes among Christians in regard to prayer. A wise Christian will avoid both. Some say that it isn't important to ask God for help with your problems and the problems of those for whom you would pray because He already knows what is best. That is a wrong attitude (Matthew 7:7, Romans 10:12, James 5:16). Others make their prayers almost exclusively prayers of petition. That is also wrong (Matthew 6:31–32). God wants us to go to Him with our problems and our needs; He commands us to pray for others, but He also wants us to go to Him with enough basic trust to know that He knows what is best and He can answer in three ways: Yes, No, Wait. That is why Jesus also said to pray, "Thy kingdom come, Thy will be done. . . ."

Let us conclude our comments on prayer with three practical don'ts. *First,* don't worry about your physical position. I think it is good to at least sometimes pray on your knees. It helps one to keep one's mind on prayer, and it puts one in a physical position of submission. However, God really doesn't care where our body is as long as our heart is in the right place. There was a man who fell into a dry well. He called and called for help but no one would come. His only resource was prayer. After he had been rescued he said that the best praying he ever did was while he was standing on his head.

Second, don't worry about your feelings. People are always saying to me, "I just don't feel that God heard me." That is nonsense. Feelings are dependent on emotions and God isn't. If you are having a particularly bad day, the chances are that when you pray you won't feel that God has heard you. God has promised that when His children pray, He hears (Proverbs 15:29). You can hang your hat on that! In fact, we are often nearer to God when we don't feel like it than when we do.

Finally, don't get discouraged. It is very easy, especially for a new Christian, to become discouraged because he isn't a spiritual giant the day after his new birth. Someone has said that discouragement is the devil's greatest tool. I haven't discussed it with him, but it wouldn't surprise me if it were true. When you feel empty, and frustrated, and tired, keep praying anyway. Why? Because God loves you!

6
How to Deal With Sin (Yours)

If we say we have fellowship with him while we walk in darkness, we lie and do not live according to the truth; but if we walk in the light, as he is in the light, we have fellowship with one another, and the blood of Jesus his Son cleanses us from all sin. If we say we have no sin, we deceive ourselves, and the truth is not in us. If we confess our sins, he is faithful and just, and will forgive our sins and cleanse us from all unrighteousness.   1 JOHN 1:6–9

Pascal once said, "If it is an extraordinary blindness to live without investigating what we are, it is a terrible one to live an evil life, while believing in God." Therein is the Christian's problem. The Christian, having been freed from the penalty of sin must, in the face of his newfound faith in Christ, do something about the power of sin. To do otherwise would be a terrible blindness because, *first*, the Christian has realized what his sin cost God. After Peter had denied his Lord three times he must have had trouble sleeping. I imagine that every time he would close his eyes he would hear the sound of a hammer driving nails into human flesh; every time he would try to sleep he would see that look of Jesus when He heard Peter's curses and denials. Peter knew what his sin cost God and from that knowledge Peter was constrained to say, "Therefore gird up your minds, be sober, set your hope fully upon the grace that is coming to you at the revelation of Jesus Christ. As obedient children, do not be conformed to the passions of your former ignorance, but as He who called you is holy, be holy yourselves in all your conduct . . ." (1 Peter 1:13–15). The Christian knows that his sin cost God His Son. Having stood on

Calvary, only the most calloused would not want to do something about the power of sin.

Second, it is a terrible blindness for the Christian to care nothing about dealing with the power of sin in his life because the same sin which cost God His Son costs the Christian the abundant life. Jesus said, "If you love me, you will keep my commandments. And I will pray the Father, and he will give you another Counselor, to be with you for ever . . ." (John 14:15). Jesus gave His followers two ways to rid themselves of sin. One is by confession and the other is by removal. To accept the first without the second is heresy. Not only is it heresy, it is hurtful. Some people think that the most miserable person in the world is Joe Pagan. That isn't true. Satan's compensations are many. The most miserable person in the world is the Christian outside the fellowship of God. That fellowship can be maintained only when sin is removed.

Third, it is a terrible blindness for the Christian to care nothing about dealing with the power of sin in his life because there is born within the life of the Christian that which propels him in the direction of godliness—an automatic pilot, if you will, that changes the Christian's wants. He now wants to do the will of God. There is a much misunderstood doctrine called The Perseverance of the Saints. That doctrine means once saved always saved, however, it means much more than that. It means that the Christian will, after coming into the experience of salvation, persevere unto salvation, that he will grow in grace, that he will manifest the fruit of the spirit i.e., love, joy, peace, patience, kindness, goodness, faithfulness, gentleness, self-control (Galatians 5:21).

Fourth, the Christian will endeavor to do something about the sin in his life simply because Jesus told him to. Jesus said, "If a man loves me, he will keep my word . . ." (John 14:23). The very fact of my being a follower of Christ means that I will want to do what He says for me to do.

Finally, the Christian will want to do something about the power of sin in his life because if he doesn't the world will think less of the Christian's Lord (Matthew 5:16). Kenneth Scott Laturette, in his monumental work, *A History of Christianity,* has listed the reasons why the Christian faith had such a phenomonal success in the first five centuries of its life despite the fact that it began as only a small, obscure sect of Judaism. Among those reasons, he points to the clear moral transformation that took place in the lives of the early Christians and which was obvious to those who took the time to notice. "Christianity worked the moral transformation which it demanded. . . . This was so frequent as to be almost normal. The apologists rang the changes on the welcome given by the Christian community to the tarnished, weak dregs of society and on the regenerating vigour of the faith." I once heard Bill Bright, founder and president of Campus Crusade for Christ, say that his daily prayer was, "Lord, help me never to do anything that would make others think less of You." If the world sees nothing in the life of the Christian which witnesses to the experience of which the Christian speaks, then the world has a right to doubt that experience.

There are three ways a Christian can deal with the power of sin in his life. The first is not very common. He can say, "Jesus took my sins to the cross, now I can do as I please." When he takes this attitude it is permissible to place him under the "doubtful" column in regard to the reality of his faith. Second, and this is the most common, a Christian can try, and try, and try to rid himself of his sin, become frustrated with the vicious circle of guilt, and give up. Time after time I have seen Christians turn away from the Christian faith because they thought they were destined to always live with the guilt. The third way is the way of Christ.

Before we discuss directly Christ's way to deal with sin some preliminary considerations are in order. First, what is sin anyway? *The Shorter Catechism of the Westminster Confession of Faith* defines sin as "any want or conformity unto, or transgression of, the law of God." To put it another way, sin is disobedience to the known will of God. This definition of sin includes both sins of commission (e.g., murder) and sins of omission (e.g., failing to love my brother). From man's standpoint there are some sins which are worse than others (a white lie versus a real whopper), but from God's standpoint sin, no matter how small or great, is a transgression which leads unto death (Romans 6:23). The person who says, "I know I'm not perfect, but

I'm better than he/she is," really doesn't understand the true nature of sin.

Second, it is important that the Christian understand the difference between temptation and sin. I may be tempted to rob a bank, but the fact that I am tempted should cause no surprise or guilt (if I truly understand my sinful nature) unless I go out and rob the bank. The Bible says that Jesus was ". . . in every respect tempted as we are, yet without sinning" (Hebrews 4:15). Later we will look at the process which leads to sin, but let it be sufficient to say here that sin proceeds from temptation but is not the same thing. Guilt is quite proper for sin, but certainly not for temptation.

Finally, the Christian should never be surprised when he finds sin in his life. The new birth is only the beginning of a process which will last your whole life. One of the reasons people are so quick to judge others is that they have not understood this principle. Suppose, for instance, that you are a naturally outgoing, gregarious person, who enjoys visiting hospitals and prisons. Now suppose that I am just the opposite in that I dislike people, don't like hospitals and prisons and am generally known as a grouch. When we both meet Christ and receive Him into our lives the change in you is going to be different than the change in me. The next day you may continue to do what you have always done and I may only smile at one person. In that case God may be more pleased with me than with you because I had much further to go than you. To remove sin from your life is not an instant happening. One of the fastest ways I know to become frustrated and discouraged in your Christian life is to fail to realize that fact.

Let us now turn to the question at hand: How do you deal with the power of sin? There are seven general rules that every Christian ought to know and observe in regard to the power of sin. *Rule one:* When the Holy Spirit reveals something to you as sin, face it and be honest about it. The Christian life is no place for rationalization. No Christian can afford the luxury of assumed goodness; he knows better. When you become aware of gossip in your life don't call it "an honest assessment of situational facts." It is sin and you ought to deal with it. When you become aware of a racist attitude in your life don't call it "an honest feeling of fear brought on by the white/black/brown people you have known." It is sin and ought to be treated as sin. When you become aware of sexual sin in your life don't call it the "natural fulfillment of physical need." It is sin and you ought to be honest about it. When you can't find it within yourself to love another person don't blame it on that person's "unlovely qualities." It is sin and God's holiness is not satisfied with a rationalization.

A classic example of rationalization and God's attitude toward it is found in the thirty-second chapter of the Book of Exodus. Moses was on Mount Sinai receiving the law from God, and the Hebrew people, because of his long absence from them, became worried. They felt that God must have deserted them. The people went to Aaron, Moses' second in command, and said, "Up, make us gods, who shall go before us; as for this Moses, the man who brought us up out of the land of Egypt, we do not know what has become of him" (v. 1). Aaron then told the people to take all of their rings of gold and bring them to him. Aaron melted the gold and fashioned it with a graving tool into a molten calf. He built an altar before it and proclaimed a feast to the new god. Now when Moses came down from the mountain he was understandably upset. When he confronted Aaron with his sin, do you know what Aaron said? "Let not the anger of my Lord burn hot; you know the people, that *they are set on evil*. . . . And I said to them, 'Let any who have gold take it off'; so they gave it to me, *and I threw it into the fire, and there came out this calf*" (vs. 22, 24). God said because of the golden calf: ". . . in the day when I visit, I will visit their sin upon them" (v. 34). Be honest about your sin!

Rule two: Remember that the Christian always deals with sin under grace and not under law. You are dealing with sin, not to keep you out of hell, but because you want to please the One who died for you. The Apostle John wrote, "My little children, I am writing this to you so that you may not sin; but if any one does sin, we have an advocate with the Father, Jesus Christ the righteous; and he is the expiation for our sins . . ." (1 John 2:1, 2). John wants us to understand that as bad as sin is, Christ has taken it to the cross. The Christian does not live under the "curse of the law." The Christian lives under the grace of God. It is important for the Christian to understand this principle because when one is going through the process of dealing with sin there is apt to be much failure. Given the natural inclination of man to sin, there must be an understanding of the love and grace of God. Without that understanding one is apt to give up altogether. Christ loves you even when you have sinned. Don't ever forget that His grace is sufficient.

Rule three: Don't be overly introspective about your sin. Satan is the accuser and he takes great delight in seeing a Christian debilitated by guilt. There are many good things about the small group movement in the church. It has provided badly needed strength and depth for the church. However, one of its dangers is an overemphasis on looking for sin. I have been a part of small groups where the general feeling has been: all right everyone, let's see how many sins we can find today. Because "the heart is deceitful above all things," we will perhaps never understand the depth of the depravity in our own lives. God's way is to deal with one thing at a time. If He revealed all of our sins at one time and said, "Now deal with them," the odds are we could not stand it. And so God is gentle with His children by giving us only as much as we can handle. A new Christian (and sometimes a mature Christian) may have a terrible battle with the so-called gross sins, but while he is dealing with those sins God doesn't usually also show him his spiritual pride and his inability to trust. When the time comes, God will bring those to his conscious mind, but until that time it is never good to probe ahead of God.

Rule four: Understand the process that leads to sin. Thomas à Kempis tells us that the process is in four steps. First, there is the bare thought of evil. (I wonder what it would be like to rob a bank.) Second, there is a strong imagination of evil. (It would be very easy to rob that particular bank because they don't have very many alert guards or smart tellers.) Third, there is delight. (Wouldn't it be wonderful to have all of the money that I could get if I should rob that bank.) And finally there is the actual act of evil. ("Stick 'em up!") Needless to say, these four steps are not always as clearly defined as the above, but most of the time one can recognize the process in situations which lead to sin. Thomas makes this observation: "Yet we must be very watchful, especially in the beginning of the temptation; for the enemy is then more easily overcome, if he be not suffered in any wise to enter the door of our hearts, but be resisted without the gate at the first knock."

Rule five: Know your weakness and live accordingly. A wise Christian will pray for his Father to reveal weakness. It is a prayer which is always answered. When it is, the information received is beyond value. The man who has a problem with sexual lust (and most men do) should stay away from *Playboy.* The woman who likes to gossip ought to be very careful when with others with the same problem. The person who has a drinking problem needs to stay away from situations where alcohol is served. The man who has not sufficiently dealt with racism in his life needs to stay away from racist literature which feeds his prejudice. Learn where your weaknesses are and then act accordingly.

Rule six: Find a friend in Christ with whom you can be completely honest, and then be honest. James says, ". . . confess your sins to one another . . ." (James 5:16). Part of the function of the family of Christ is to minister to each other in the matter of sin. It is important that you find at least one other member of the family who can help and guide you. Confession is good for the soul. Just be very careful to whom you confess. Obviously, you shouldn't pick the town gossip or a "day-old" Christian. Find someone who will not condemn you and who has enough maturity to be truthful and loving at the same time. You will find that if just one other brother or sister knows you completely, it will be easier to live with yourself with objectivity. The advisor will be able to see things you can't see, to give advice which would be difficult to take from a stranger and impossible to obtain for yourself. Many Christians have found this kind of ministry can be mutual between two Christians.

Rule seven: Remember that the Christian faith is not a do-it-yourself religion. Jesus said, ". . . apart from me you can do nothing" (John 15:5). The Christian who doesn't understand this is headed for dismal spiritual failure. Anyone who has tried to be good, pure, righteous, loving, kind, and honest by himself knows that it can't be done. When you are aware of sin in your life don't assume that the battle is won. It has only begun. Ask Christ not only to make you aware of your sin, but also to enable you to overcome it. The Bible says, "No temptation has overtaken you that is not common to man. God is faithful, and He will not let you be tempted beyond your strength, but with the temptation will also provide the way of escape . . . (1 Corinthians 10:13). Again the Bible says, ". . . for God is at work in you, both to will and to work for His good pleasure" (Philippians 2:13). Claim those promises for your life. Ask God to do that which He has promised, and He will. The only people on the face of the earth for whom Christ can do anything are sinners—sinners who know it and who want to do something about it.

7
How to Deal With Sin (Others)

Judge not, that you be not judged. For with the judgment you pronounce you will be judged, and the measure you give will be the measure you get. Why do you see the speck that is in your brother's eye, but do not notice the log that is in your own eye? Or how can you say to your brother, "Let me take the speck out of your eye," when there is the log in your own eye? You hypocrite, first take the log out of your own eye, and then you will see clearly to take the speck out of your brother's eye.

MATTHEW 7:1–5

Brethren, if a man is overtaken in any trespass, you who are spiritual should restore him in a spirit of gentleness. Look to yourself, lest you too be tempted. GALATIANS 6:1

Thomas à Kempis has written, "The inward Christian preferreth the care of himself before all other cares. And he that diligently attendeth unto himself, easily keepeth silence concerning others. Thou wilt never be thus inwardly devout, unless thou be silent concerning other men's matters, and look especially to thyself. If thou attend wholly unto thyself and God, thou wilt be but little moved with whatsoever thou seest abroad." Thomas has given us one of the basic principles of the Christian faith: The sins of other people, especially the sins of Joe Pagan and Jane Cynic, are not our concern. In dealing with our own sin, you and I have our hands full.

One of the most terrible images Christians have communicated to the world has been the image that we are saints whose main mission in life is to point out the sins of those who aren't saints. Nothing could be further from what Christians ought to be. A Christian ought to know that the circumstances of any particular person's life are largely unknown. Given the same circumstances and the human bent toward evil, the wise Christian knows that he might be in exactly the same position of sin. As a minister I, perhaps more than other people, have access to the secret and hidden side of a number of people's lives. I have found that things are rarely as they seem. The boy on drugs, the girl who is pregnant out of wedlock, the man who is an alcoholic, the woman who is always so angry, are people whose circumstances, and burdens, and hurts are different from mine. It is only by God's grace that their sins are not my sins, and I have no right to judge.

The Christian, if he has taken the time to read the Bible, knows that pure motives are hard to come by. Jeremiah said, "The heart is deceitful above all things . . ." (Jeremiah 17:9). In other words, it is only in very exceptional cases that one does evil for purely evil reasons or good for purely good reasons. Usually our motives for doing what we do are so clouded and confused that we never completely understand them. For that reason the Christian is very slow to praise himself and very slow to condemn others.

The Christian knows that he is what he is (a child of God) by God's grace. When he became a Christian it was not because he was good enough, or righteous enough, or pure enough—it was because God loved enough. "While we were yet helpless, at the right time Christ died for the ungodly" (Romans 5:6). I have come into the experience of salvation and I am held there because God loves me in spite of my sin. The Christian who has watched God's Son die for him will be very slow to judge others because the Christian knows that he isn't good enough!

Also, the Christian will be slow to condemn others for their sins because, very simply, Jesus told him not to. Our attitude toward other people is a matter of obedience. Our younger daughter is not allowed to go out to the end of a pier where we sometimes swim. She is too young to understand what it means to drown; she doesn't understand death; she doesn't know that some people can swim and others cannot, but she won't go to the end of the pier because she knows what it means to be obedient to her parents. Her reason for not going to the end of the pier has nothing to do with water safety. It is just a matter of obedience. The Christian knows that what Jesus says for him to do or not to do is best. Jesus said not to judge other people!

The Bible is very clear about the necessity of silence in the face of the sins of others. However, there are four exceptions to this general principle: (1) when we are witnessing to someone about their need of Christ; (2) when our responsibility to others makes it necessary to stand clearly against certain kinds of sin (e.g., racism); (3) when one Christian is helping another; and (4) when someone else's sins cause us to be bitter and resentful. We will discuss the first two exceptions in later chapters (number 1 in chapter 11, and number 2 in chapter 12). Let us turn to the last two.

What is our responsibility to a brother or sister in regard to their sin? Before we look at that responsibility let me give you a word of caution. Most of the time your responsibility for sin stops with the end of your nose. There are some Christians who believe their God-given ministry is the ministry of pointing out the sins of their fellow Christians. Everyone has known the sister who has launched a personal crusade to get brother George to stop smoking, or the brother who has decided that God has told him to keep sister Hildegarde from wearing short skirts. That kind of Christian needs someone to deal with him! Only God knows the number of Christians who have turned from the walk of faith because a brother or sister took out his or her hostility and hurt in the form of judgment. Beware of that Christian who prefaces his or her remarks by saying, "Now, what I am going to tell you is for your own good. . . ." Beware of becoming that kind of person yourself!

However, even with that word of caution there are times when Christians should deal with the sins of other Christians. James tells us: "Therefore confess your sins to one another, and pray for one another, that you may be healed" (James 5:16). Christians have a responsibility to other Christians and that responsibility does not end in the matter of sin. The Apostle Paul gives us the method by which a Christian ought to deal with another Christian's sins. "Brethren, if a man is overtaken in any trespass, you who are spiritual should restore him in a spirit of gentleness. Look to yourself, lest you too be tempted" (Galatians 6:1). Here Paul has given us three requirements that must be met before we speak to another Christian's sin problem.

The first requirement is spirituality. When Paul says that those who are spiritual should deal with another's sin he means those who are walking filled with the Spirit. A Christian who is out of fellowship with God (chapter 3) has no business even thinking about the sin of another. But Paul means more than that. He is also talking about spirituality in particular areas. I have only known a few Christians (and I had my doubts about them) who could say that they had no problem with sin. Most of us, if we are serious with God, have achieved by His grace some measure of victory in particular areas. When we have achieved victory over a particular area of sin in our lives, then we are enabled to help someone else who is having a problem *in that same area.* For instance, I know a man who is a shining example of how God can deal with the problem of alcoholism. He has been "on the wagon" for almost twelve years. However, he still has a problem with anger. Whenever, during counseling, I encounter an alcoholic problem he is the man I call. He knows what he is doing and he is in fellowship with God. Now if I came across someone who wants help with his temper, this man would be the last man I would call. He is spiritual in a general way (filled with the Spirit) and he is spiritual in a particular area (alcoholism) and thus meets the first qualification given by Paul.

The second qualification is gentleness. May God save us from the narrow, negative, and nauseating Christian whose critical spirit is more obvious than God's Spirit. One of the fruits of the Holy Spirit is gentleness (Galatians 5:22). Gentleness implies a mildness and a lack of harshness that can communicate love. One of my pet peeves is the great increase in attendance at the Christmas and Easter worship services of the church. The first year I was in the ministry, on Easter Sunday, after a winter of very poor attendance at the services, I looked into the sanctuary before the worship service and noticed that it was packed and that the ushers were putting up chairs. My anger was so obvious I had to go into my study to calm down. In my study I paced back and forth thinking of the number of ways I could "fix" those terrible pagans who came only on Easter. The janitor in the church walked by the study and noticed that I was about to do something I would regret later. He came into the room and closed the door behind him. "Sit down," he said. I sat. "Stephen," he said, "I understand how you feel. There are times when I have felt that way myself, but you have to remember that you can't talk about God's love with the kind of anger you are expressing right now. Besides," he went on, "you may never get another chance to talk to these people again, so don't blow it." He smiled as he got up and left the study. His gentleness with my sin of harshness and anger was something I will never forget.

The third requirement is humility. Paul tells us that we should look at ourselves, lest we acquire the same sin we are trying to deal with in others. Paul is saying that no Christian can go to another Christian with the assumption of exemption. The Christian who is aware of his own weakness without the grace of God will always deal with the sin of others with a gentle and loving hand. It is the only way to communicate to another more than judgment and condemnation.

It is necessary, sometimes, for Christians to deal with the sin of other Christians. First, it is necessary because all Christians are hurt when one Christian's witness is marred by sin. Just as one crooked policeman can hurt all policemen, one carnal and obviously sinful Christian can hurt another Christian's witness for Christ. Second, Christians need to deal with the sin of other Christians for the same reason mountain climbers scaling a high mountain must help each other. It isn't a question of one man climbing the mountain and another not making it. It is a question of the need for helping one another or no one will make it. You can't be a Christian by yourself because you need other Christians who can help you deal with your sin. When Christians are in fellowship with Christ, when they are gentle with one another and when there is humility and love, there can then be honesty. It is that kind of honesty which will give power to the Church of Christ.

The second exception to the rule of nonjudgment which is appropriate to this discussion is when someone else's sin against you causes you to be bitter, angry, and/or resentful. In reality, that is your sin and not theirs, but because it involves another person there is the necessity of dealing also with the sin of another. Jesus, in the fifth chapter of Matthew gives us some basic principles.

> You have heard that it was said, "An eye for an eye and a tooth for a tooth." But I say to you, Do not resist one who is evil. But if any one strikes you on the right cheek, turn to him the other also; and if any one would sue you and take your coat, let him have your cloak as well; and if any one forces you to go one mile, go with him two miles. Give to him who begs from you, and do not refuse him who would borrow from you. You have heard that it was said, "You shall love your neighbor and hate your enemy." But I say to you, Love your enemies and pray for those who persecute you, so that you may be sons of your Father who is in heaven; for He makes His sun rise on the evil and on the good, and sends rain on the just and on the unjust. For if you love those who love you, what reward have you? Do not even the tax collectors do the same? And if you salute only your brethren, what more are you doing than others? Do not even the Gentiles do the same? You, therefore, must be perfect, as your heavenly Father is perfect.
>
> MATTHEW 5:38–48

First, Jesus is asking the Christian to face the fact of his own anger and resentment. One of the dangers in being a Christian is that you often hear the admonition that you are supposed to love everyone. It is natural for a person to try and become what others say he ought to become, and having failed that, to fake it. In other words, there are many people who say they love a particular person (and may even think they do) but who, in reality, harbor deep resentment and hostility toward that person. Jesus, in giving us this teaching, is saying that it is important for a Christian to admit and face the fact of sin in general and, in this passage, resentment in particular.

Second, Jesus tells us that we must love the person for whom we have feelings of hate and bitterness. Notice that Jesus doesn't say we are to tolerate our enemy or to get along with our enemy—He says that we are to love him. Therein is the difficulty. How do you love someone who doesn't love you? How do you love the unlovely? How do you love someone who has hurt you? The Christian has a way and Jesus speaks of that way when He says, ". . . for He [God] makes His sun rise on the evil and on the good, and sends rain on the just and on the unjust" (Matthew 5:45).

You can't love until you have been loved and then you can only love to the degree to which you have been loved. God loved you when you were unlovely; He loved you when you were not just; He went to a cross when you were too evil to deserve it. When you have been loved to that degree you are able to love. When the resentment swells up in you, meditate on the cross of Christ. You will be surprised by the difference it will make.

Third, Jesus tells us that we are to pray for the person for whom we have resentment. If you are a Christian and you don't have a prayer list which includes the people who cause you to be resentful, then you are missing one of the great helps God has given to the Christian. It is hard to hate the person for whom you are praying. You start by being honest with God about your resentment, and by telling Him that you don't even like praying for the person. Before long you find that you don't mind praying for him. Later you will discover that you have lost your resentment.

Fourth, Jesus said that we should do something for the person for whom we hold resentment. I once heard a story about a Christian young man who joined the army and found himself in the barracks with probably the worst group of pagans who ever lived. They laughed at him and made fun of his Christian faith. One evening he was kneeling beside his bed praying when one of the other soldiers came back to the barracks drunk. When he saw this young man praying he took his heavy army boots off and threw them at the praying Christian. The next morning the soldier who had thrown the boots found those same boots beside his bed shined and polished! When someone has sinned against you and you find the anger and the resentment welling up inside, do something good for that person for his sake, for your sake—and for God's sake. (Sometimes doing something for another person who has caused you resentment means going to him and talking about the problem, and confessing your part in the hurt. However, it is sometimes better to not talk unless you can honestly face the fact of your sin of resentment.)

Johan Bojer, the late Norwegian novelist and playwright, in *The Great Hunger*, tells of a man whose child was killed by a neighbor's dog. A famine came in the land, and the man who owned the dog had no corn to plant in his fields. The man whose child had been killed by the dog went and planted corn in his enemy's field. He explained, "I went and sowed seed in my enemy's field that God might exist. . . ."

8
How to Know God's Will

I will instruct you and teach you the way you should go; I will counsel you with my eye upon you. PSALMS 32:8

God is not in the business of keeping His will from us! To hear some people talk you would think He was. "If only I knew God's will," a woman told me recently, "then I would feel better about the direction of my life." Jesus said, "Whoever does the will of God is my brother, and sister, and mother" (Mark 3:35). Most Christians want that kind of relationship, but they don't know what the will of God is, much less how to do it. Time and time again I have heard Christians express the fear that they were not in the will of God. "I have prayed day and night about my future," a college student said, "and if God knows what He wants me to do, He is sure keeping it a secret from me."

In this chapter I want to show you how to know the will of God, but before we look at the principles involved it is necessary to dispense with two preliminary considerations. First, if a Christian is to be clear about what God wants, that Christian must be clear about wanting what God wants. I once overheard a frustrated mother of a teen-ager (most parents of teen-agers are) say to a friend, "I just don't tell him what to do anymore. He won't do it anyway." I would suspect that God must feel like that sometimes. God, the Bible tells us, sees us ". . . not as man sees; man looks on the outward appearance, but the Lord looks on the heart" (1 Samuel 16:7). We may appear to others to be earnestly seeking God's will, but if we really aren't, God knows it. Some-

73

times God must say, "I don't tell him what to do anymore. He won't do it anyway."

One of the major reasons a lot of Christians don't get any fresh word from the Lord is because they don't want to hear the word. The Lord may tell them to do something they don't want to do; He may tell them to love someone they don't want to love; He may want them to serve where they don't want to serve. Before one prays for God to reveal His will, one ought to pray for God's grace in order to want to do God's will. Jesus said, ". . . if any man's will is to do his will, he shall know . . ." (John 7:17).

The second preliminary consideration will save you a lot of needless worry and trouble. It is this: If you are in fellowship with God and if you are living the Christian life by God's grace, it is safe to assume that you are in the will of God. Because God doesn't try to keep His will from us, if He wants us to do something different from what we are doing with our lives, He will tell us. Too many Christians are paralyzed in their Christian life because they are continually waiting for God to reveal His will. When I was in commercial broadcasting and working for a rock station, the cardinal sin was "dead air" (i.e., silence). One thing I heard often was, "Don't just stand there! Do something!" That's good advice for the Christian. If you are reading and applying Scripture to your life, you have plenty to do that you know to be the will of God. Don't continually ask God to show you something else. There just may not be anything else.

God does sometimes lead a Christian to go to Africa, but most of the time He tells us to go next door. He sometimes gives us specific instructions for a great work, but most of the time He expects us to do the work He has given us in the life we are living. There are certainly times when God calls a Christian to a different field of service, but most of the time He wants us to be a teacher, or truck-driver, or housewife, or mother, or businessman, or tradesman, or secretary, or student, according to His will and for His glory. What you are doing right now is probably where God has called you (until He lets you know different) and what you are doing now, because it is the will of God, should be done as service to Him.

Now to the subject at hand: How do you know the will of God?

There are five ways for a Christian to know the will of God. Let's look at them. *First, God reveals His will to the Christian in the Bible.* The Bible is very clear about what the duty of the Christian is. God's will for the Christian is never left in doubt in certain specific areas. Not too long ago a man who was having an affair with his best friend's wife came to me with a strange statement, "I am trying to discern God's will in this matter." Well, that should not have been too difficult! God is very specific about His will concerning adultery.

The Bible has some clear teaching on God's revealed will. The Christian should know, for instance, that it is God's will for him to be a witness to others about Christ. When Christ says, "Go and tell," and the Christian is sitting and watching, the Christian is not doing the will of God. It is God's will that we should be reconciled to our brother. If we aren't, we are not doing His will. The Bible lets us know how God feels about murder, and stealing, and racism, and anger. The Bible defines love and what it should do in our lives. If we don't find the kind of love the Bible describes in our lives then we are not doing God's will. One way, then, to know God's will is to listen to what the Bible plainly says about it. That is the reason it is important for the Christian to read the Bible daily.

Another way God uses the Bible to reveal His will to the Christian is by bringing to mind Scripture we have read and remembered. Many Christians will testify to the importance of Bible memorization. The Christian ought to have a regular program of memorizing Scripture verses so that God's Word can be used by God in particular circumstances. I have a friend who is a television announcer in Boston. He has a lot of free time between commercials and station breaks. He uses that time to memorize Scripture. Some Christians have Scripture verses written on small cards and they carry one of the cards with a Scripture verse on it with them all day. Whenever they have the opportunity, they read it, committing the verse to memory. Some businessmen I know use their lunch hour to memorize Scripture. Some busy mothers keep a verse of Scripture before them in the kitchen and whenever they have a chance they look at it trying to commit it to memory. Why do these Christians think that it is important to memorize Scripture? Because time after time when they were hurt, or lonely, or afraid, or doubtful, God has brought just the right word to them because He had the tools with which to work. In specific situations God leads Christians by calling to mind certain passages of Scripture—when they are there.

Another way God reveals His will with Scripture is by emphasizing a particular verse or sentence in the Scripture while we are reading it. Every Christian, if he has been reading the Bible very long, knows the experience of reading a passage of Scripture (perhaps even a very familiar passage) and having the words leap off the page. That is the Holy Spirit emphasizing a special communication from God. I have a friend who in regular Bible study was reading from the twenty-fifth chapter of Matthew about the final judgment. In that passage Jesus says that all the nations of the earth will be gathered before Him and He will separate them into two groups. One group will be commended because they fed the hungry, gave drink to the thirsty, took in strangers, clothed the naked and visited those who were sick and in prison. The other group He will send away into eternal punishment because they didn't do those things. Jesus tells His listeners that when they do these works to the least of His brethren they do them to Him. My friend, I suppose, had read these words a hundred times. But on this particular occasion he was especially taken by them. Very soon after the Holy Spirit brought those words to his attention, he was asked to help in a prison ministry. It was clear what God wanted!

The second way God leads the Christian is in prayer. A good rule for the Christian is: When in doubt—ask. Prayer puts us in the proper position for guidance—the position of obedience. Prayer makes us open to God's will. Prayer puts us into contact with the only One who knows for sure what should be done. In the quietness of prayer God speaks often in the "still small voice" making clear that which He wills.

Madame Chiang Kai-shek once wrote, "My mother was not a sentimental parent. In many ways she was a Spartan. But one of my strongest childhood experiences is of Mother going to a room she kept for the purpose on the third floor to pray. She spent hours in prayer, often beginning before dawn. When we asked her advice about anything, she would say, 'I must ask God first.' " If you are seeking God's will in a particular area and you haven't done any serious praying about it, then God must assume that it isn't too important to you anyway.

The third way God leads is by circumstances. I have a friend who believes that God is calling him into the ministry. However, he has a problem. His wife can't stand the thought of his being a minister. She is very happy in their present life and doesn't believe God is leading them anywhere except where they are. My friend told me that if God wanted him in the ministry He would have to change his wife's mind because in a decision that important it would be necessary for both he and his wife to be committed together. He is a wise Christian. He knows that circumstances often reveal God's will.

The Bible says, ". . . there are varieties of gifts, but the same Spirit . . ." (1 Corinthians 12:4). That means that under circumstances one ought to list God-given abilities. For instance, God didn't call me to be a farmer. Perhaps my view of farming is overidealized, but I can think of nothing I would rather do than be a farmer. (Some of my friends who are farmers say that I would be cured of that desire with just one day behind a plow.) My problem is that I can't get even a flower to grow. I can just look at my wife's African violets and they die. One time a few years ago I tried to get some roses to grow. I bought the best roses you could buy; I got a book on how to grow roses; I followed the instructions precisely. When I planted those roses I planted them so they would get a proper amount of sun. I watered them daily and made sure they were getting the right fertilizer. Do you know what happened? Those roses didn't even try. They died without growing even a single leaf. I am sure God didn't call me to be a farmer because I just don't have any abilities in that area.

Under circumstances one ought to consider feelings. After Saint Francis had been called by God one of his particular areas of concern was among the lepers. Always before, Saint Francis had been repulsed by the sight of leprosy, but God gave him a wonderful love for lepers almost immediately after his conversion. It is clear that God was calling Saint Francis to that kind of ministry. I have people in my church who would rather visit in nursing homes than do anything else. Others are interested in working with drug addicts. Some of the members have a special interest and ability in evangelism. One man has the ability to carry on a prison ministry. It is safe to assume that God is calling these people to work in specific areas because of their feeling for those areas of ministry.

Let me give you a word of caution here. Be careful that you don't use feelings as an excuse to do nothing. God doesn't always call a person to do that which is the most enjoyable or the most desirable. Sometimes God wants us to do things that are not what we would do if we had a choice. Usually, God, if we are obedient to Him, gives us the necessary love once we act according to His will, but not always. That is why feelings should never be the determining factor in our discerning God's will for our lives. Feelings are only one indication of what God wants for us and should always be balanced against the other methods God has given us.

Fourth, God uses other Christians to reveal His will to us. Sometimes God will speak to us through another Christian just so we will remember that the Christian faith is a team effort. In the twenty-first chapter of Acts we have an example in the actions of Paul. After the Apostle Paul's first missionary journey, after hundreds of Gentiles from Tarsus to Corinth had been led to a saving faith in Christ Jesus, Paul traveled hundreds of miles back to Jerusalem to check it out with the other Christians there. The question which was bothering Paul was how a Gentile ought to live the Christian life in what had before been a largely Jewish movement. The advice Paul received from his brothers in Jerusalem constituted God's will.

The late Sam Shoemaker has spoken to this point, "Truth is the tonic of fellowship. It keeps it from becoming soft and squashy. We all have a general idea that fellowship is wonderful and we want it very much, but sometimes we are not willing to pay the cost of it. The cost is chiefly the willingness to go through the pain of giving and receiving the corrective of truth. We put ourselves out of fellowship in two ways —by refusing to be honest with others when we see them doing a wrong thing, or a right thing in the wrong way; or by refusing to receive from them the same tonic honesty as to our own needs." In fellowship with other Christians God has given us the corrective that is needed in discerning His will.

Now that doesn't mean that you have to be obedient to everything said by other Christians. A Christian should have enough wisdom to be open to what other Christians say and also enough discernment to know when to be closed. I know some Christians who are against every proposal which comes before them on the general principle that if it is new, or different, or bold, it must be wrong. You ought to be very careful about discerning God's will in that kind of Christian's advice. Half of the time (if the law of averages is correct) they are going to be wrong!

But be that as it may, there are some brothers and sisters with whom I am very close. When they speak I listen; when they give advice I weigh it very carefully; when I am in doubt about a certain course of action I rely on their advice. God has given the Christian the gift of Christian fellowship. He didn't give us that gift so that we could smile at each other and tell each other how nice we are. He gave fellowship to us so that in the hard decisions of life, in the enterprise of God's work, in the conflicting currents of the world's concerns we would have a place of understanding, and correction and advice. Obedience to the Body of Christ (our brothers and sisters in Christ) is often the same thing as obedience to God!

Finally, God sometimes tells the Christian what to do directly. I know a pastor who was driving by the home of a parishioner one afternoon when he had an overwhelming feeling that he was supposed to stop. He was very busy at the time and so he drove on by. But the feeling became stronger until a few blocks away he had to turn around and go back. He felt silly as he approached the door of this elderly lady's home. She came to the door and invited him in and they sat down with a cup of coffee. Soon the conversation turned, for a reason the pastor couldn't explain, to the subject of death. For over an hour they discussed the promises God had given Christians concerning death. The next day this same woman had a stroke and was completely paralyzed for a week unable to communicate with anyone. At the end of the week she went home to be with her Lord. She was able to greet death with peace because one man had been sensitive enough to obey God's direction.

Now most of the time God doesn't lead the Christian this way. One ought to be very careful about that brother or sister who gives the impression that he or she has a special hot line to God and that God uses the line often in giving specific instructions. God's will is usually communicated in one or all of the first four ways we have discussed. God never forces His will upon us. Most of the time He gives us time to think and reason and test. But there are occasions as in the above incident, when God speaks, and it is hard to ignore what He says.

Sir Ernest Shackleton has expressed what can be the experience and testimony of every Christian. When he returned to England to report on his Antarctic explorations, he told the king: "Bending above the oars, struggling through the snow, battling across the ranges, always there was Another. He made the difference between triumph and disaster. He brought us through!"

9
How to Deal With the Devil

Be sober, be watchful. Your adversary the devil prowls around like a roaring lion, seeking some one to devour. Resist him, firm in your faith, knowing that the same experience of suffering is required of your brotherhood throughout the world.   PETER 5:8,9

An acquaintance of mine was recently visiting some friends when the subject of God came up. One of the men joined in the conversation with the assertion that he didn't believe in God. My friend replied, "Jim, tell me the kind of God you don't believe in; I may not believe in that god either." There are a lot of people who don't believe in the devil, and many of them don't believe in him for the same reason others don't believe in God. Their ideas are immature. I don't believe in a god with a long white beard who sits on a cloud. I don't believe in that kind of a god for the same reason I don't believe in a devil who carries a pitch fork, has a long tail and runs around in a weird red suit.

I do, however, believe in a devil because I have seen him. I have seen him walking down the streets of a city slum; I have watched him do his work with a needle dripping heroin; I have seen him in a bottle clutched in the hand of a drunk who had fallen asleep on a bench on Boston Common. I have read his handwriting in a suicide note. I have seen him smiling as the crowds lined up to watch an "adult" movie. I have seen the work of Satan in a crushed automobile, and an empty stomach, and a dead soldier. I have seen Satan in the words of a man who said he didn't need God, and in the sneer of a woman who was

81

asked if she knew Christ. I have seen Satan in the hurt, and emptiness and frustration of humanity. Sometimes I see him in my doubts, and my anger and my fear.

In this chapter I want to introduce you to some information which will be ignored only with dangerous results. The information is about a personality so evil that most people can't even comprehend the depth of that evil. In this chapter I want to introduce you to a being who is as evil as God is good, as selfish as God is unselfish, and as hateful as God is loving. His name is Satan and he cares about you!

The writers of the Bible don't mind talking about Satan at all. He is called the liar, the accuser, the dragon, the serpent and the ruler of the world. As one reads what the Bible says about the work of Satan it is enough to make any believer pause. Satan is the tempter who would lure the believer away from the walk of faith. He seeks to destroy God's Word in the experience of the believer. He is an accuser who would cripple the Christian with guilt and fear. He sometimes becomes regnant in an individual life. Satan is responsible for sin and unbelief and he rejoices whenever he can turn a pagan away from Christ, and a Christian away from the Christian life. He would have you fall down and worship him even if you call him by another name. He is real; he is alive; and he is dangerous.

Perhaps the clearest teaching we have on this being of absolute evil comes from the lips of Jesus Himself. When Jesus saw the unbelief of many so-called religious people He said, "You are of your father the devil, and your will is to do your father's desires. He was a murderer from the beginning, and has nothing to do with the truth, because there is no truth in him. When he lies, he speaks according to his own nature, for he is a liar and the father of lies" (John 8:44). Jesus pointed to Satan as the reason some people refuse to accept God's Word: "The sower sows the word. And these are the ones along the path, where the word is sown; when they hear, Satan immediately comes and takes away the word which is sown in them" (Mark 4:14). Jesus called Satan the "ruler of this world" (John 12:31). And when Jesus wanted to give Peter something to hold on to after Peter would deny Jesus, Jesus predicted that denial with these words: "Simon, Simon, behold,

Satan demanded to have you, that he might sift you like wheat, but I have prayed for you that your faith may not fail; and when you have turned again, strengthen your brethren" (Luke 22:31, 32). Time after time Jesus warned His disciples about the dangers of Satan.

Now you may still have difficulty in believing in a real and personal devil. (If there was a devil, however, he would be very happy if he could keep you from believing in him.) If that is your situation don't skip this chapter! You need the information too much. Just substitute the words *metaphorical personification of evil* everytime you see the word *Satan* or *devil.* Your designation, I believe, will be wrong, but the ammunition will be effective nevertheless. A lion by any other name will be just as dead when you shoot him with a gun as a lion who is properly called a lion.

Before we look at the ways God has given the believer to deal with the devil, let me give you two preliminary considerations which will be helpful. *First,* there are three sources of a believer's temptation and his sin: (1) the world, (2) the flesh, and (3) Satan. It is important for a Christian to diagnose the source of his temptation properly.

For instance, a Christian may have a problem with gambling. Suppose he goes to a poker party and afterward complains that Satan tempted him to gamble. Now Satan may have played a part in it, but that man was tempted more by his own weakness and the lure of the world than he was by Satan. It is easy for a person to blame Satan for his own weakness. That kind of cop-out does nothing but cause immaturity in the Christian because honesty is God's tool for growth. Every time you fail, every time you sin, every time you refuse to do the will of God don't say (with Flip Wilson's Geraldine), "The devil made me do it." Even if he did, that does not remove your personal responsibility. Even if he did, the main source of your problem may still be your leaving yourself open to him by indulging in your weakness (flesh) or by being involved too much in that which is not of God (world).

Second, it is important for the Christian to remember that Satan is a defeated foe (Colossians 2:15; Revelation 20:10). The Christian is playing in a ball game that has been fixed. The contest has already been decided! The victory has already been won! Satan will come out on the short end of the stick! You can count on it because on the cross of Christ Satan's end was secured.

"So, if Satan is a defeated foe," you might ask, "why do I still have so much trouble with him?" The problem is appropriation. In other words we have not internalized that which has already been done for us. Suppose I had a very rich aunt who lived in another state and she should die and leave me a million dollars. Suppose further that I didn't know she had died and that I didn't know about my inheritance. I may be very poor in my ignorance about the million dollars, but I would be very rich *in fact*. In order to turn my poverty into wealth I would have to know the facts of the matter and then appropriate the money (i.e., go to the bank and get it) for myself. Many Christians are ignorant of the victory over Satan which was won for them on the cross. Because of that ignorance they have never appropriated it for themselves.

God has given the Christian five ways to deal with Satan—five ways to appropriate for ourselves that which has already been done for us in fact. Our inheritance only needs to be collected if we go about it properly. *First,* there is *prayer.* When Jesus taught His disciples how to pray He said that they should pray for the Father to deliver them from the evil one (Matthew 6:13). The Greek of the Lord's Prayer could be better translated, "deliver us from the evil one," than "deliver us from evil." When Jesus was in the garden of Gethsemane and His disciples couldn't stay awake during His moment of agony, Jesus told them, "Watch and pray that you may not enter into temptation . . ." (Matthew 26:41).

The Christian has at his hands a vast amount of potential power. Prayer is the only key that will open the storehouse of that power. The Apostle Paul wrote, ". . . we are not contending against flesh and blood, but against the principalities, against the powers, against the world rulers of this present darkness, against the spiritual hosts of wickedness in the heavenly places" (Ephesians 6:12). That is a frightening picture! If you feel that you understand it, you are on dangerous ground. With our finite minds it is very difficult, if not impossible, to even comprehend the "principalities," "powers," and "hosts of wickedness." However, the Christian has access to One who does understand and who can, therefore, do battle with the enemy and win. The Christian who does not avail himself of that access is very foolish.

When temptation comes the Christian's prayer should always be: "Father, I don't understand the power that is against me for evil, but You do, and You have promised help. I now claim the victory that You have already won for me on the cross." When you encounter Satan get on your knees and pray. Then when you turn to do battle with Satan you may find no one is there. John Bunyan was right: "Pray often; for prayer is a shield for the soul, a sacrifice to God, and a scourge for Satan."

The *second* method God has given the Christian to appropriate the victory already won is *faith*. In the sixth chapter of Ephesians Paul gives the Christian a list of weapons he will need when doing battle with Satan, ". . . above all taking the shield of faith, with which you can quench all the flaming darts of the evil one" (Ephesians 6:16). If you remember, we have said before that faith isn't something which springs full-blown in the Christian's life. Just as you have to nurture a rose, so you must nurture faith to see it grow.

Another word for faith is trust, and it takes time to learn to trust. The closer and the longer the Christian walks with Christ the more the Christian will see Christ working in his life. That walk will build trust and from that trust will flow a confidence in the ability of Christ to deal with anything that happens—including Satan. Satan has already been defeated and he knows it. Faith is when the Christian knows it too!

Third, the Christian aids in the appropriation of Christ's victory over Satan with *watchfulness.* The Bible says, "Be sober, be watchful. Your adversary the devil prowls around like a roaring lion, seeking some one to devour" (1 Peter 5:8). Because the reality of Satan is often thought to be myth and because, in a sophisticated time, we don't believe in "wizards that peep and mutter" anymore, it is easy for even the Christian to decide that he has too many real problems to confront without having to think about something seemingly so remote as Satan. That is a terrible mistake. Marshall W. Fishwick in his book, *Faust Revisited: Some Thoughts on Satan,* points to the problem of people who underestimate the power of Satan. His advice: "No one who does go out should underestimate the task. Evil is active, eternal, omnipresent, contagious. We must expect to encounter it wherever we go, whatever we do. Satan never sleeps; he never even rests on his arms. When we think he is gone he is most there. When we are proudest we most readily betray ourselves."

One of the safety slogans used quite often is: DEFENSIVE DRIVING SAVES LIVES. That slogan is applicable for the Christian life. Don't assume that you are too spiritual to be attacked by the tempter (nobody is); don't think that because you have read your Bible and prayed that you are now free from the possibility of evil (nobody is); don't think that there is some magic formula which will exempt you from the devil's plans (there isn't). The closer you draw to Jesus the closer Satan will try to draw toward you. If you know that, you will be watchful. After almost every spiritual victory in your life you will be open to depression, doubt, pride, anger, and evil thoughts. (If you do what the evil one wants you to do, he will have no reason to bother you.) To be forewarned is to be forearmed!

Fourth, in order to appropriate the victory which was won for you on the cross be prepared to *resist.* The Bible says, "Resist him [the devil], firm in your faith, knowing that the same experience of suffering is required of your brotherhood throughout the world"(1 Peter 5:9). The Apostle James has given us a clear promise in this regard: "Submit yourselves therefore to God. Resist the devil and he will flee from you" (James 4:7). One of the most dangerous heresies for any Christian is the belief that one need do nothing to resist evil because Jesus does it all. Now there is a real sense in which Jesus does do everything. Any Christian living the Christian life knows, as he looks back on his experience, that Jesus called him, and led him, and empowered him, and changed him. However, within the experience itself a Christian must resist.

Now I want you to notice that I didn't tell you to fight the battle yourself or that your heroic effort would have to be that which defeats Satan. That isn't what the Scriptures mean when they talk about resistance. If they did we would not be able to do anything. Have you ever seen those displays of cans in a supermarket which are arranged so that if someone accidentally removes one can from the bottom of the arrangement the whole display will fall in a pile? Well, to resist Satan is to remove that one can. The resistance you offer is the symbol which will bring to your aid all of the power necessary to defeat Satan. Satan flees not because you have resisted. He flees because he knows that your resistance is that which enlists the mighty power of God's legions.

The man who is tempted by Satan to commit adultery, for instance, can very easily yield to that temptation. But when he resists, when he says to himself, "I will not indulge myself in even the thought of an act so harmful to me and my family," he will find that something strange happens to him. He finds that the mere act of resistance provides a power he didn't know he had. He finds that he isn't the only one doing the resisting. He finds that ". . . he who is in you is greater than he who is in the world" (1 John 4:4).

The *final* method of appropriation is the use of *truth*. When Paul is talking about how a Christian ought to resist Satan he says, "Stand therefore, having girded your loins with truth . . ." (Ephesians 6:14). Again he says, "And take the helmet of salvation, and the sword of the Spirit, which is the word of God" (Ephesians 6:17). In other words, Paul is saying that there is a way to counter lies and that is with truth. If someone tells me that my mother doesn't exist, how do you think I would answer that person? I certainly wouldn't compose a philosophical treatise on the subject of the existence of mothers and the existence of my mother in particular. I would point to the fact of my existence and then very simply explain about the birds and the bees. I would have him taste some of my mother's banana pudding. I would take him and introduce him to my mother. The truth would be a very effective weapon in dealing with so foolish a doubt. It is the same way with the Christian faith. God has given the Christian a body of truth (the Scripture) with which he can counter lies.

If Satan tries to tell me that I do not belong to Christ (which is one of his favorite games) I will quote John 1:12. If he tells me that my weakness will cause me to fall beyond the love of Christ I will quote John 10:27, 28. When I tend to think that the temptations I face will be so strong that I will have no way out I will remember 1 Corinthians

10:13. When I can't sleep at night because I am afraid of death I will get out my Bible and read John 14 and 1 Corinthians 15. When I am in danger of judging the spiritual depravity of my fellow man I will think about Ephesians 2:8, 9. When the burdens of just keeping on keeping on get to be too much and I think that no one cares I will read again Psalms 55:22. There is no substitute for the truth, and there is no truth more useful to the Christian in his battle with Satan than the truth of Scripture. In my battle with Satan, no matter how strong he seems, I will remember the truth: "He [God] disarmed the principalities and powers and made a public example of them, triumphing over them in him [Christ]" (Colossians 2:15). That's a fact, and I will stand on it!

10
Christians Are Human Too!

My grace is sufficient for you, for my power is made perfect in weakness.
CORINTHIANS 12:9

In this chapter I want to talk to you about what I believe to be one of the major problems Christians face. It isn't a problem for Joe Pagan and Jane Cynic, but to the person who wants to live the Christian life, the problem assumes major proportions. The problem is this: Most Christians, even though they sometimes don't admit it, fail to really see their weakness clearly. But more important than that, most Christians fail to see their weakness in relation to God's strength. Because of this failure many Christians live a life of frustration and guilt. God doesn't sell frustration and guilt in His store! If you have them, you didn't get them from Him! Let's talk about it.

Not too long ago a man came to see me who was one of the most miserable-looking individuals I have ever seen. As we talked I discovered that he had been making some very important promises to God. He had promised that he would give his life wholly and completely to God. He had promised that at every opportunity he would be a faithful witness for Jesus Christ. He had promised that in all of his actions he would be clean and pure. He had promised that he would burn himself out for God.

Now, those were laudable promises, and I am sure God heard them and was pleased. However, there was a problem. As this young man tried to live his life, as he got out into the daily grind of just keeping on keeping on he found that no matter how hard he tried he couldn't keep his promises. There had been times when he knew he should have witnessed for Christ, but on those occasions he had decided that silence was better and easier. He had not been absolutely pure and righteous. He had not really burned himself out for God—in fact, he had hardly gone near the flame. And now, because he had failed so often, he came to tell me that he was giving the whole thing up.

There are thousands of Christians just like this man who have a strong desire to follow Christ wherever He should lead, and yet, who want to give it up when they find they aren't strong enough, or good enough, or spiritual enough. God has just demanded too much, they say, and the impossibility of the whole enterprise either makes for hypocrites or failures. In this chapter I want to tell you some of the things I told this man. The information contained herein is important because it is Biblical, and because all Christians need, on occasions, to be reminded that they are human.

The root of the difficulty is quite simply this: Most of us feel that God can't do without us—if we fail, God fails. We have all heard the poem by Annie Johnson Flint which expresses this idea:

> Christ has no hands but our hands
>   To do His work today;
> He has no feet but our feet
>   To lead men in His way;
> He has no tongues but our tongues
>   To tell men how He died;
> He has no help but our help
>   To bring them to His side.

Balderdash! That is one of the greatest lies ever perpetrated on the Christian community. Everything doesn't depend on you, and the sooner each Christian learns that truth the better. One of the reasons Jesus formed the Church was to make up the difference between what individuals ought to do and what they do.

Somewhere, perhaps from those of us who don't make clear exactly what the Christian life involves, some new Christians (and some older ones) have gotten the idea that when they become a Christian they somehow become superhuman, and if they don't see superhuman qualities in their life they feel they must not really be a Christian. Nothing could be further from the truth! In his position of new life the Christian is, in fact, a completely new creature. There is now the power to do and will many things which were not possible before. However, that does not mean that all of a sudden the Christian is not human anymore. Spiritual depression, failure, hurt and sin are still possible in the Christian, and a feeling that none of these things should ever happen to a Christian makes them seem even more real. When you stick a Christian with a pin, he bleeds just like everyone else. If a Christian jumps off a ten-story building he dies just like everyone else. Some Christians do have financial problems, family problems and health problems. Time after time I have heard Christians say, "I thought I was a Christian, but I know now that I was just being idealistic." In other words, they are saying, "I thought I was perfect, but now I know I'm not." The danger is in equating being perfect with being Christian. If you have been doing that, I have some very good news for you: Christians are human too!

Listen to what one of the finest Christians who ever lived, the Apostle Paul, had to say about physical problems: "And to keep me from being too elated by the abundance of revelations, a thorn was given me in the flesh, a messenger of Satan, to harass me, to keep me from being too elated. Three times I besought the Lord about this, that it should leave me; but he said to me, 'My grace is sufficient for you, for my power is made perfect in weakness' " (2 Corinthians 12:7–9). What Paul is saying in these verses is that Christians are just as weak physically as other human beings.

The things I am going to say about physical problems may not apply to you right now, but I want you to take note because it is important to be prepared for physical problems before they happen. When I was in seminary in Boston the papers were filled with stories of the great Alaskan earthquake. We asked one of the seminary professors what he would say to his congregation on Sunday morning if he was a pastor in Alaska. We wanted to know how you explain that much suffering and loss to Christians. He answered, "If I were a pastor in Alaska, I would not have to say much. I would have prepared them for tragedy before tragedy happened." His answer was wise.

The good news the Bible has for Christians who suffer from physical problems is that God knows and understands. No matter how much pain you suffer, no matter how tired you get, no matter how weak you are, God knows that you are an "earthen vessel" and He will love you and use you anyway. Catharine Booth said that she could not remember a time in her life when she was without pain. Beethoven was the son of an alcoholic and became deaf at the age of twenty-eight. When Handel wrote the *Messiah* he was suffering from a paralyzed right side and right arm. Ignatius Loyola suffered from lifelong pain. Fanny Crosby was blind. And we could go on and on. The point is this: Your physical weakness is not a sign of God's disfavor; it is that which God has promised to help you overcome and use.

I believe God does perform miracles of healing in our time. Any pastor can give you incident after incident of God's healing power. But to say that, is a far cry from saying that God's healing is given as a reward for goodness, or piety, or spirituality. The Christian life is not a life of power without pressure. It is power *under* pressure! That includes the pressure of physical weakness. One of the great dangers involved in the resurgence of interest in spiritual healing in our time is the danger of those who aren't healed feeling that the fault lies within themselves. That just isn't true. Helen Keller said on one occasion that she thanked God for her handicaps because through them she had found herself, her work and her God.

I don't know what your physical problem is right now, or what it will be in the future. Sometimes, God in His grace sees fit to provide healing—but sometimes He doesn't. Whatever He does is best for you and should not cause guilt because His "grace is sufficient for you," and His "power is made perfect in weakness." Sickness can be God's gift as much as health.

But Christians are not only weak physically, they are still human in regard to sin. Now what I say here should not be misunderstood. I am not saying that sin is OK. I am not saying that because it is human to sin it is all right to sin. John and I have the same goal: "My

92

little children, I am writing this to you so that you may not sin; but if any one does sin, we have an advocate with the Father, Jesus Christ the righteous; and he is the expiation for our sins . . ." (1 John 2:1, 2).

Again let's look at the words of the Apostle Paul: "I do not understand my own actions. For I do not do what I want, but I do the very thing I hate. Now if I do what I do not want, I agree that the law is good. So then it is no longer I that do it, but sin which dwells within me. For I know that nothing good dwells within me, that is, in my flesh. I can will what is right, but I cannot do it. For I do not do the good I want, but the evil I do not want is what I do" (Romans 7:15–19). And we say, "Now wait a minute, Paul. You're supposed to be Paul: super-Christian. You are an apostle. You wrote much of the New Testament. You were the first Christian missionary. You certainly don't mean that you still had a problem with sin after all that. You certainly don't mean that you fell short of God's demands." If Paul were here I am sure he would say, "That's exactly what I mean!"

One of Satan's (again, if you don't believe in Satan you may substitute *metaphorical personification of evil*) greatest tricks is to say to the Christian who has sinned, "Ah, you've done it again. You have done all that talking about being such a dedicated Christian. You aren't any more a Christian than I am a Christian. How could you be a Christian and act as you do? You aren't a Christian—you are a hypocrite." And then the Christian says, "You know, you're right. I'm not a Christian." May God forgive us for falling into that trap. It is a worse sin than the one which caused the dialogue in the first place.

Let me give you the spiritual cycle in which many Christians live. They promise God that they will follow Him no matter what, and they sincerely try—and fail. Then they say to themselves, "I have tried and failed therefore I'm not worthy (which is precisely the point)." Then the Christian is hesitant to go before God because of the sin, and becomes spiritually dead. But in the midst of the deadness the Christian realizes that he can't live without God and so he goes to God and starts the whole process again. The good news of the Christian faith is that that kind of cycle is a lie. The Christian is the person who, more

93

than anyone else, realizes his own imperfection and depends on Christ alone to make up for it. That kind of dependence removes guilt and provides power (chapter 6) to overcome the sin.

There was a small college in the Midwest which used to advertise that it was seven miles from any known sin. Would to God that it were true! I would go there and live the rest of my life. But our sin isn't so much outside us, is it? It is part of us, and that is why it hurts so much. God has provided the power to overcome the sin about which you are aware right now. The chances are that when you have, by His grace, overcome it, He will show you other sins with which you must deal. Dealing with sin is a lifelong process. Guilt over that which is a part of your nature isn't necessary for the Christian. That's the reason for the cross. There are just two kinds of people in this world: those who are sinners and don't know it, and those who are sinners and know it and are trying to do something about it. The Christian is of the latter breed. It isn't getting in the mud that is the worst part. (That's part of being human.) It is staying there!

Christians are not only human physically and in regard to sin, they are also human spiritually. Listen again to the words of Paul: "For we do not want you to be ignorant, brethren, of the affliction we experienced in Asia; for we were so utterly, unbearably crushed that we despaired of life itself. Why, we felt that we had received the sentence of death; but that was to make us rely not on ourselves but on God who raises the dead . . ." (2 Corinthians 1:8, 9). Someone said to me recently, "Steve, since I became a Christian, I have never lost the sense of God's presence." People, that man was either a fool or a liar or both. Why? Because as the Bible says, we are earthen vessels. Because we are earthen vessels we sometimes live on the spiritual mountaintop, but sometimes we must go through the valley of despair and darkness so that we might appreciate the mountaintop.

You are probably saying right now, "All right, I understand that my spiritual depression is normal, but that doesn't help me much when I am going through it. What I want to know is what can I do about it? How can I get rid of it? I will tell you: Praise God anyway! Continue with your prayer life anyway! Read the Scripture anyway! Serve and witness anyway! And, for God's sake, don't whine about how you have lost everything because you are going through a period of spiritual depression. You haven't. You're just human.

Physical weakness, spiritual weakness, and sin are a part of the Christian life because Christians are human too. But let me tell you something else. God's strength is not dependent on your weakness. Aren't you glad? Let's look again at the words of the Apostle Paul: "But we have this treasure in earthen vessels, to show that the transcendent power belongs to God and not to us. We are afflicted in every way, but not crushed; perplexed, but not driven to despair; persecuted, but not forsaken; struck down, but not destroyed; always carrying in the body the death of Jesus, so that the life of Jesus may also be manifested in our bodies. For while we live we are always being given up to death for Jesus' sake, so that the life of Jesus may be manifested in our mortal flesh" (2 Corinthians 4:7,8).

I am very pessimistic about human nature. I call it realism (some would say cynicism), but I'll tell you something: whereas I may be pessimistic about man, I am extremely optimistic about God and what He can do with and through weak and sinful men and women who are willing to let Him. That's the only kind of people He has with which to work. He knew that before He created us and called us unto Himself. He requires only that we follow Him. He knows that we will fail physically, that we will sin, that we are weak spiritually. If He is willing to allow us to follow Him anyway, that should be enough. Nothing depends on our strength. If it did, God's work would go undone. Nothing is dependent on our purity. If it did we could forget about God ever doing anything in the world. Nothing depends on our spirituality. If it did, the Christian faith would be a farce. You are nothing, and I am nothing outside God's grace. The world doesn't rest on our shoulders; it rests on God's shoulders. John Wesley was right: "God buries the workmen and goes on with His work. Hallelujah!"

Let's allow Pascal to sum up: "Christianity is strange. It bids man recognize that he is vile, even abominable, and bids him desire to be like God. Without such a counterpoise, this dignity would make him horribly vain, or this humiliation would make him terribly abject."

11

How to Share Your Faith

*All authority in heaven and on earth has been given to me. Go therefore
and make disciples of all nations. . . . and lo, I am with you always, to
the close of the age.*   MATTHEW 28:18–20

*Always be prepared to make a defense to any one who calls you to
account for the hope that is in you, yet do it with gentleness and rever-
ence. . . .*   1 PETER 3:15

Jesus' commandment for His followers to share their faith with
others was not an optional commandment. He didn't say, "Go and
make disciples when you feel like it, or when you have nothing better
to do." He said, "Go therefore and make disciples . . ." (Matthew
28:19). He also said, "Follow me and I will make you become fishers
of men" (Mark 1:17). He said further, "But you shall receive power
when the Holy Spirit has come upon you; and you shall be my
witnesses in Jerusalem and in all Judea and Samaria and to the end
of the earth" (Acts 1:8). It is clear to anyone who spends any time
at all reading the Bible that the main task of the Christian is the task
of sharing his faith. When the Christian gets to heaven, the Father is
going to want to know who the Christian brought with him!

However, even with such clear directions from our Lord Himself,
most Christians are not actively sharing their faith with anyone. Most
Christians will give witness to their golf game before they will give
witness to their Lord; most Christians are more interested in what
others think of them than in what they think of Jesus; most Christians
will share a recipe before they will share the joy that comes only from

Jesus; most Christians are active conversationalists until someone starts talking about God. A good question which ought to be faced by all who belong to Christ is this: Where would the Body of Christ be right now if everyone shared their faith as I am sharing my faith? Or to put it another way: Would our Christian family even be in existence right now if our brothers and sisters in the past shared their faith the way we do in the present?

While I believe that most Christians are not actively sharing their faith in Christ, I don't believe that the reason is a lack of desire. The problem is that many Christians have accepted as truth three of the greatest lies ever told. Let's examine those lies. The *first* is this: People don't want to hear about Christ. "Every time I speak of my faith," a man told me, "I feel that I am imposing." Another person told me recently, "You're always talking about witnessing about our faith. Well, you just don't know my friends. They are busy, active people and the last thing they are interested in is my faith."

Now let me tell you the truth. There was probably never a time in history when people were more open to the answers to life which are given in the gospel than now; there was probably never a time in history when people were more desperately searching for someone who believes something that makes a difference than now. If we don't ever talk about what we believe, if we never mention the answers we know, those people will not be impressed by our tolerance or our tact. They will just think we don't have any answers.

If you had cancer and there was someone who had a cure and refused to share it with you, what would you think of that person? We live in a time when the cancer of emptiness, and frustration, and guilt, and loneliness, and boredom can't be covered any longer. For most people the old ways of forgetting don't work anymore, and they know it. Only the hurt remains. If someone, anyone, can speak to that hurt they will listen.

I have an acquaintance who often spends his lunch hour on the Boston Common. One day he decided that he would test out the myth that no one wants to hear about Christ. He started by going up to someone on the common, starting a conversation and finally talking about Jesus. After only a few weeks he had won over nineteen young people to Christ. These are his words: "Not everyone received Christ, but all were interested and all listened." If what you have in Christ is real and you aren't ashamed to talk about it, you will be surprised at those who will listen—especially those you thought were too busy or too active to care.

The *second* lie is this: One must be very good before one can speak about Christ to others. A man said to me, "Steve, you're asking me to talk about Christ. I would feel like a hypocrite. I'm not good enough." If you wait until you are good enough to talk about Christ, you never will! Goodness is not the prerequisite for sharing your faith! Your witness is not to your goodness but to the goodness of Christ. Your witness is not to your purity but to a God who loved you even when He knew that your "purity level" was low.

Peter's Pentecostal sermon in the second chapter of Acts was not preached because Peter felt he was pure enough to preach it. It was preached against the background of denial and cowardice. What if Peter had said, "Fellows, I know there are a lot of people here in Jersualem who need to know about Jesus, but, don't you remember, I denied even knowing Him. I'm certainly not the one to do the preaching." Peter didn't say that. In spite of his imperfections he had something to say about a God who loved him even knowing about his denial. Because he said it, almost three thousand people came to know Christ.

The Christian's witness is not from the position of goodness. If it were it would be a dishonest witness. No one would listen either, because they would figure that the Christian faith was only for good people. The Christian's witness is from the position of one who, in spite of his sinfulness, has been found by a God who has forgiven and accepted the sinner.

The *third* lie believed by a great number of Christians is the lie that one must know enough before talking about Christ. They believe that one must be well trained in theology and the Bible before one should even attempt to talk about Jesus. Listen, if you wait until you know enough, you will never share your faith with anyone. In fact, one of the prerequisites for success in witnessing is an overwhelming sense of inadequacy. What do you think would have happened if after Jesus gave the great commission Peter had raised his hand and said, "Lord, I'm only a fisherman. Don't you think we should establish a seminary before we go out making disciples? We just don't know enough." If that had happened, if that had been the attitude of any of the disciples the Christian faith would never have gotten off the ground. If that is your attitude, you won't either.

If a friend comes to you with a request for five dollars you don't have to be an expert economist before you can give it to him. You wouldn't say, "Look, I would like to give you the money, but I just don't understand the international monetary system." Just as your complete understanding of a monetary system is not the prerequisite for giving money away, your complete understanding of the Christian faith is not the prerequisite for giving your faith away. One time Jesus healed a man who had been born blind, and the authorities could not accept the miracle. They called the blind man to come before them and said, "Give God the praise; we know that this man [Jesus] is a sinner." He answered, "Whether he is a sinner, I do not know; *one thing I know, that though I was blind, now I see*" (John 9:24, 25).

You may not understand the hermeneutical principles involved in the interpretation of Scripture (you may not even know what *hermeneutical* means) but you can talk about what you do know. You can say, "I was empty, now I am filled; I was afraid, now I have found courage; I was lonely, now I have a Friend; I was not loved, now I am loved; I was guilty, now I have been forgiven; I was lost, now I have been found; I was bound, now I am free; I was blind, now I see!" If you have experienced anything in Christ, you can talk about it and you can live it. That is sharing your faith.

Now let's turn to the subject at hand, how to share your faith. Before one can share something with someone else, it is important that there be a clear understanding of what is to be shared. The content of the gospel is very specific and it is very important. (I would suggest that you reread chapter 2 for a review of that which needs to be shared.) For instance, one of the problems with many Christians is that they only talk about God's love. As important as that is, if the love is not seen against the background of God's justice and our sin, then the talk is not talk about the gospel. To speak of man's sin

100

without speaking of God's grace is not to speak about the gospel; it is to speak only of problems. To speak of heaven without speaking of judgment is to be dishonest.

The gospel presentation ought to contain the following facts: (1) Man is a sinner and separated from a righteous, just and holy God (Romans 3:10, 23; Galatians 3:10). (2) God is a God of love who wills that none should perish or be out of fellowship with Him (John 3:16; 2 Peter 3:9). (3) God offers to man the abundant life, but that life comes only from Him as found in Jesus Christ (John 10:10). (4) God's only remedy for man's sin and separation is the cross of Christ where God took man's sin and placed it on Christ who died in our place reconciling man to God. (Romans 5:8, 11; 2 Corinthians 5:19; John 14:6). (5) In order to come into a relationship with Christ we must acknowledge our sin and trust in Christ alone for our salvation (Mark 2:17; John 1:12; Revelation 3:20).

Before a Christian attempts to share his faith it is important that the above facts are clear. The first time anyone asked me how to become a Christian, I gave him a book. That should never have happened. It would have been quite simple to relate to him these facts, check to see if he understood them and asked him, right then, to pray the "receiving" prayer for Christ (i.e., Father, I come before You knowing that I am a sinner and deserve nothing from You. But right now, accepting Your promise of forgiveness, I confess my sin and invite Christ to come into my life. From this moment on, my life is Yours and I will, by Your grace, be Your faithful disciple until my life's end. I now thank You that You have honored Your promise, and that Jesus is my Saviour and Lord. Amen). Christians miss so many opportunities to speak to others about Christ because when the opportunity comes along they just don't know what to say. Learn what to say and say it. You'll be glad you did.

It is important also, that the Christian understand the proper motivation for sharing Christ. Too many Christians try to lead others to Christ so they might add another "scalp" to their Christian belt. Too many Christians are only faithful in sharing their faith so that they might say to their brothers and sisters, "Look at me. I'm super-Christian. I have won twenty people to Christ without losing even one." May God forgive that kind of motivation. God sends us out to talk about Jesus and that is the reason we should do it. God is love and He commands us to love our neighbors. That is why we should share Christ. God has given us a faith that won't keep unless we give it away. That is why we should share Christ. Any motivation that is not the proper motivation will not be honored by God.

I know a man whose Christian commitment is as real and vital as any I know. His problem was that his wife was not a Christian. He had repeatedly tried to lead her to the kind of faith which had become a reality in his own life, and he had repeatedly failed until he realized his motivation. He wanted her to be a Christian because others wondered why such a fine Christian man should have a wife who didn't know Jesus. He wanted her to be a Christian because as long as she stayed out of the family, it made him look bad. When he realized his motivation, and confessed it to God and to his wife, everything changed. His wife, for the first time, realized what he had been talking about and turned to Christ in faith. Her name is now recorded in the Book of Life because he got his motivation in line with Christ.

But not only is motivation and content important when you talk to another about Christ, the position from which you witness is just as important. The Christian, having been accepted and loved by God, must now go to others only as one beggar telling another beggar where to find bread. One of the worst public relations fiascos ever caused by the church is the way the church has given the impression that it is made up of good people who are in the business of making everyone else good—and miserable. Somewhere Joe Pagan and Jane Cynic have gotten the idea that we are coming to them with the message: "Look how great, and pure, and good, and committed we are. We want you to be that way too." The world won't buy that for two reasons: First, because they know it is a lie; and second, because they have enough problems already.

The Scripture says, "For by grace you have been saved through faith; and this is not your own doing, it is the gift of God—not because of works, lest any man should boast" (Ephesians 2:8). Remember that before you ever talk to anyone about Christ! You should go to another, not because you are so good and committed or even because you were so wise to accept what Christ offered. We should always share Christ in the realization that He came to us when we couldn't come to Him, that He loved us when we couldn't love Him, that He has given us life when we couldn't obtain it for ourselves. Anything less than that, any attitude other than that will serve only to misrepresent Christ and your faith!

It is also important for the Christian to realize that if anyone comes to know Christ as the result of our witness it will only be because the Holy Spirit was operating in the situation. Before we witness we ought to be sure that we are filled with the Holy Spirit (chapter 3). Before we speak to others about their sin, we must always speak to God about our sin; we should confess our sin and ask Him to once again fill us with His Spirit. Unless that happens before we talk to others about Christ, their knowing Christ will depend on our ability and talent in presenting Him. That means, for all intents and purposes, that no one will.

Also, it is important for the Christian to spend some time talking to God about the person to whom the witness is directed. When possible that person ought to be lifted before God in prayer by name, asking God's Spirit to intervene, to take our poor presentation and use it to glorify Christ. The rule is this: Before talking to our friends about Christ, we should talk to Christ about our friends.

Finally, the Christian's concern should not be for results. Our responsibility is to share Christ; what happens after we have done that is God's concern. Someone once asked a missionary, who had been serving for twenty years in a remote outpost with only two converts to Christ, "What in the world do you stay for?" The missionary replied, "I am here because God put me here. What He does with me and my work is His business, not mine." One of the best definitions I know for successful witnessing is the definition used by Campus Crusade for Christ: "Success in witnessing is simply sharing Christ in the power of the Holy Spirit and leaving the results to God."

Christ has called you to witness. Half of the battle is deciding that you are going to be obedient to that call. Tell God that you are willing to talk to others about Him, if He will just open the door and let you know when it is open. Don't tell God that unless you really mean it, because He will take you at your word. Every Christian who is serious about wanting to share his faith will find countless opportunities to do so. I can promise you that—so does God.

12

The Christian's Responsibility

What does it profit, my brethren, if a man says he has faith but has not works? Can his faith save him? If a brother or sister is ill-clad and in lack of food, and one of you says to them, "Go in peace, be warmed and filled," without giving them the things needed for the body, what does it profit? So faith by itself, if it has no works, is dead. JAMES 2:14–17

Thus far in this book we have been talking primarily about God's free grace given to a sinner who doesn't deserve it. We have seen that salvation comes by faith and not by works. We have seen that there is nothing, absolutely nothing, anyone can do which will buy salvation. When you became a Christian it had nothing to do with your goodness, your purity, your lovable qualities. We have seen that your relationship to Christ, once established, has nothing to do with what you do either before or after. Being saved means trusting in Christ *alone.* As far as your relationship to Christ is concerned, nothing depends on you. Everything depends on God who came to you when you couldn't come to Him, who called you by name when you didn't know His name. "For by grace you have been saved through faith; and this is not your own doing, it is the gift of God—not because of works, lest any man should boast" (Ephesians 2:8, 9). Nothing I say in this chapter should be taken to mean that any of the above is not true.

Now if you have properly understood the doctrine of Justification by Faith in Christ, then there is a good chance that you have some questions: Why even try to be good enough to please God when you are not justified by works but by faith? Would it not be better to sin more so that grace might abound more? Since we can never be good enough to please God with our goodness, why try? If a man is justified by faith, why bother to be good, or pure, or honest, or loving?

One of the most dangerous traps into which a Christian can fall is the trap of assuming that because he is saved by faith he doesn't have to do anything else. John the Baptist, who certainly could not be described as the most tactful man who ever lived, one time exploded with these words, "You brood of vipers! Who warned you to flee from the wrath to come? Bear fruits that befit repentance, and do not begin to say to yourselves, 'We have Abraham as our father'; for I tell you, God is able from these stones to raise up children to Abraham. [Gentiles may translate that sentence: "Bear fruits that befit repentance, and do not begin to say to yourselves, 'We are members of the church and our fathers were officers in the church'; for I tell you, God is able from these stones to raise up church members whose fathers have been church officers."] Even now the axe is laid to the root of the trees; every tree therefore that does not bear good fruit is cut down and thrown into the fire" (Luke 3:7–9). Jesus was somewhat milder in tone, but His message was the same: "Are grapes gathered from thorns, or figs from thistles? So every sound tree bears good fruit, but the bad tree bears evil fruit. A sound tree cannot bear evil fruit, nor can a bad tree bear good fruit. Every tree that does not bear good fruit is cut down and thrown into the fire. Thus you will know them by their fruits" (Matthew 7:16–19).

I once heard a teen-ager say in response to an invitation to come to a Youth for Christ rally, "No thank you. I don't buy it. My parents don't buy it either." He was asked about his parents because they certainly were substantial members of the community and the church. His reply: "They talk a lot about God, but it doesn't mean a thing. They just keep on fighting and putting their nickel in the collection plate. Whenever my dad wants to make a fast buck he does it in any way he can. He doesn't mind hedging a little on his tax report either. They don't buy this Jesus stuff and neither do I. I'm just honest about it." That young man had a point.

One time G. Campbell Morgan, one of the greatest Bible expositors in the history of the church, was speaking to Dwight L. Moody about the importance of the Bible to national life. Dwight L. Moody replied, "Oh, yes, the nation needs the Bible; but take it from me, the Christian man is the world's Bible. . . ." You see, Joe Pagan and Jane Cynic don't care too much about "God talk" unless they see some real "God action." They know that drugs and booze will help them forget the rut in which they live. If you don't have anything better than that which you can demonstrate with your life, then they would rather you just keep quiet.

There is a song my oldest little girl has just learned which makes a point:

> If you're saved and you know it shout "Amen."
> If you're saved and you know it shout "Amen."
> *If you're saved and you know it.*
> *Then your life should really show it.*
> If you're saved and you know it shout "Amen."

If you are saved and you know it, *why* should your life really show it? Your life should show it because you now have a natural desire to please Jesus who died in your place. One of the marks of a good marriage is the desire on the part of the partners in that marriage to please the other. If that desire isn't there then there is no real marriage. Someone tells about a young artist who painted a picture of the Last Supper. He took the picture to Tolstoy for his criticism. After he had examined the painting, Tolstoy pointed to the central figure in the painting and said, "You do not love him." "Why," said the young artist, "that is the Lord Christ." "I know," replied Tolstoy, "but you do not love him. If you loved him more, you would paint him better." It is the desire of the real Christian to please the One he loves. If we loved Him more we would live for Him better.

Second, our life should really show our relationship to Christ because that relationship, by its very nature, is a relationship of obedience. There is no question, for the Christian, about God's will concerning gossip, or lying, or stealing, or murder. Jesus is very clear about our relationship to other human beings. Racism, hate, and anger are excluded from the life of the Christian insofar as the Christian is able, for the same reason dirty boots are excluded from the makeup of a marine. The word is *obedience*.

Third, our life should really show our relationship to Christ because the natural outgrowth of the indwelling Christ is the life which manifests goodness, and temperance, and love, and joy, and purity. When Methodist ministers are ordained they are asked, "Are you moving on to perfection?" That's a good question because it points to the normal Christian life. The Christian who says, "I am going to be good if it kills me," often finds that it does. However, the Christian who is in fellowship with Christ finds that, almost without knowing it, he is getting better, and purer, and kinder, and more loving for the same reason a rose blooms. A rose blooms because it is a rose. A Christian moves on to perfection, because he is a Christian.

Now let's become a little more specific. If you are saved and you know it, *how* should your life show it?

First, your life should show forth a spiritual quality that is different. The closer you draw to Christ, the more others will notice a change in you which can't be attributed to your good works or your personal morality. When you draw near to Christ, others begin to notice. I once served a church where over one winter a group of laymen in the church got very serious with God. They decided that together they would allow Christ to deepen their lives. These people, along with their minister, grew spiritually in ways I never thought possible. Over that winter one of the members of that church went to Florida. When he returned in the spring, he came up to me after a morning service and said, "Pastor, something is different around here. Your sermon was the same; the choir was the same; the building hasn't changed. But this morning there was something fresh and real in this service that I have never felt before." That man was feeling and knowing the presence of Christ in that small group of people whose lives radiated a quality that was different and real.

As the Christian deepens his spiritual life prayer and Bible study become easier and more real too. When someone first becomes a Christian, I often tell them to set aside only five minutes a day for prayer and Bible study (two-and one-half minutes for prayer and two-and one-half minutes for Bible reading) because much more time than that sometimes is frustrating for a new Christian. However, after a person has been a Christian for a while he finds that he can't do it in five minutes. In fact, an hour of prayer and Bible study a day isn't enough. As the Christian grows in his or her spiritual life, the reality of Christ is more important. A dentist in my congregation said recently, "I used to be a part of the church because it was important to me. Now I can honestly say that I can't live without Christ." A real estate man said, "The church as an institution at one time in my life was the most important thing in the world. Now Christ is." As a Christian grows spiritually, the deep and hidden truths of the Scripture begin to become clear. The Bible speaks to people at different levels. It has something for the new Christian and something for the mature Christian. As one deepens spiritually God's truth as revealed in His Word becomes more clear.

When all of these things happen to the Christian there is an X factor that begins to be noticed by others. Witnessing takes on new power, a word spoken to comfort is more sincere, life seems more real. During the great revival in Wales in 1904 in which 100,000 were converted, the man who was used by God as His instrument for revival was Evan Roberts, a twenty-six-year-old student. It is said that often when he would walk down the aisle of a church men and women would come under conviction and receive Christ. Many times he didn't even have to preach! What do you suppose was happening? The depth of his life which was in Christ provided a real spiritual witness beyond his words or his actions.

Second, the personal morality of the Christian should be such that others see the difference. A retired minister once told me, "Steve, never live your life so that others will know that you are a minister. But if they find out, don't let them be surprised." That is good advice for any Christian. Live your life in such a way that if anyone finds out that you are a follower of Christ, they won't be surprised. How do you think Christ would have you decide on the movies you attend? What kind of language do you think Christ would use? Where should you draw the line in your relationships with the opposite sex? Does God condone adultery? Are drugs OK for a follower of Christ? What about alcoholic beverages? Should you be honest in a school exam, or a business deal, or an income tax report? What about integrity in your work or in your family life? How does your life measure up against the Ten Commandments (Exodus 20) and the Sermon on the Mount (Matthew 5–7)? Etcetera, etcetera. The problem with many Christians is not that they don't know what they ought to do in regard to their personal morality. The Bible is usually very clear in most areas (contrary to what a number of people say); the question is one of finding out what God says, and doing it.

Let me add a word of clarification here. The personal morality revealed in the Scripture isn't given to us to keep us from having any fun. God isn't in the business of trying to make the Christian as miserable as possible. He wants us to have the abundant life (John 10:10). He gives us standards because they will increase our happiness, not lessen it. He reveals standards of conduct for the Christian because those standards are the best, the easiest, and the finest way to live. He has revealed standards of conduct for the Christian because there are laws that are in the very nature of things—laws which can't be broken without paying a very great price. Someone has said, "The devil says, 'Take what you want, and pay for it.' "

Finally, (and here is the place where many Christians have a blind spot) the Christian's responsibility to others (social morality) ought to be such that non-Christians see the difference. I was just on the phone with a girl of fourteen who was into drugs. She came to me some time ago to say that she was frightened and weak. I talked to her about Christ and suggested that she should find some Christian friends quick. I sent her to a Bible study and prayer group in which a number of former drug users are involved. She told me on the phone, "Pastor, I was afraid to go at first because I thought they would be examining me to see if I was good enough. But they accepted me right off. It is the best thing that has ever happened to me. Now, when I am tempted to take drugs, I know there are people who are Christians and who would be disappointed if I did!" That young lady had found friends who took seriously their social responsibility as Christians.

The Christian has a responsibility to share Christ (Matthew 28:19), a responsibility to love others (Luke 6:27) and a responsibility to show compassion (James 15:16). It is absolute spiritual blindness when any

Christian talks about drinking, and smoking and sex without ever talking or thinking about racism, and poverty, and civil rights, and war. You see, racism is just as great a sin as is sexual immorality. To turn one's back on the hungry, the lonely, the hurt, the afraid, the poor, the imprisoned, the naked is just as great a sin as dishonesty. When Jesus said that fruit should be the criterion for measuring the reality of faith, He was including the fruit that is seen in a Christian's relationship to others.

The Bible says, "He who says he is in the light and hates his brother is in the darkness still. He who loves his brother abides in the light, and in it there is no cause for stumbling. But he who hates his brother is in the darkness and walks in the darkness, and does not know where he is going, because the darkness has blinded his eyes" (1 John 2:9–11). When a lawyer once asked Jesus what he should do to inherit eternal life, Jesus pointed to the love of God and the love of neighbor. When the lawyer persisted in asking who his neighbor was, Jesus told the story of the good Samaritan who helped a man who had been beaten by robbers when two so-called religious people had refused to help. Jesus then asked, "Which of these three, do you think, proved neighbor to the man who fell among the robbers?" He said, "The one who showed mercy on him." And Jesus said to him, "Go and do likewise." (Luke 10:36, 37) It is interesting to note that of the nine fruits of the Holy Spirit given in the fifth chapter of Galatians (i.e., love, joy, peace, patience, kindness, goodness, faithfulness, gentleness, self-control) six are clearly to be understood only in relationship with others.

In a book titled, *Dreams and Dream Life,* published a number of years ago, Olive Schreiner has this passage: "I thought I stood in heaven before God's throne, and God asked me what I had come for. I said I had come to arraign my brother man because he is not worthy, and my hands are pure. I showed them. God said, 'How is this?' I said, 'Dear Lord, the streets on earth are full of mire. If I should walk straight on in them my outer robe might be besotted, you see how white it is! Therefore I pick my way.' God said, 'On what?' I was silent, and I let my robe fall. I wrapped my mantle about my head. I went out softly. I was afraid that the angels would see me."

13

What Difference Does the Church Make?

For where two or three are gathered in my name, there am I in the midst of them.   MATTHEW 18:20

Husbands, love your wives, as Christ loved the church and gave himself up for her . . . that he might present the church to himself in splendor, without spot or wrinkle or any such thing, that she might be holy and without blemish.   EPHESIANS 5:25–27

Some Christians believe that when they come to know Christ that is all there is to it. We have all heard, and maybe even said ourselves, "My religion is something only between me and God. It is no one's affair but mine!" If you feel that way, then you need to read this chapter very carefully because you are in for a surprise. The Bible teaches that when you became a Christian you passed the entrance requirements for the church. In fact, not only have you passed the entrance requirement, the Bible says you are already a member of the church. To say that your religion is your business and no one else's is like saying, "My marriage is a private affair. It has nothing to do with my wife." To speak about the Christian faith without any reference to others who are Christians is like a businessman saying, "How I conduct my business is my business. It has nothing to do with my employees, or my product, or my customers." The Christian faith is not a private matter. It involves your brothers and sisters. When that involvement takes place you call it the church.

Before we go any further let's examine the word, *church*. There is a lot of misunderstanding about the word because people have used it outside the Biblical context. Sometimes people talk of the church as if it were a building, or a good thing for the community, or a group of quasi-religious people who have come together to talk about God. But the Biblical word for church means none of these things. The Greek word used in the Bible is *ecclesia,* and it means "called-out ones." Also, the Bible calls the church "the Body of Christ," "the Bride of Christ," and "the Family of God." These terms would define the church, not just as an organization, but as an organism. That organism works out its presence, I believe, in the institution of the church. But there is a difference, and an important difference between the organism and the organization.

And so my brother and sister, you became a member of the church when you received Christ as your Lord and Saviour. The question is not whether or not you are a member; the question is whether or not you are going to fulfill your obligation as a member. You became a part of your fleshly family when you were first born. You became a part of your spiritual family (i.e., the church) when you were born the second time. In both cases you can walk away and reject your family, but you can't in either case cease to be a part of the family—albeit a bad part.

And so when a Christian asks the question of this chapter, what difference does the church make, that question is not asked so as to decide whether or not to be *in* the church. That is already an accomplished fact. The question when properly understood, is asked in order to perceive one's place in the church.

Before we discuss the importance of the church (i.e., the difference the church makes) it is important that we discuss more deeply what exactly the church is. Before an individual can answer the question of purpose or experience, there is the prior question of essence which must be answered. In other words, we can't understand what we are doing here unless we first know who we are. That is true also of the church. We can't understand what difference the church will make unless we know what the church is. It is important to examine some of the Biblical points as to the definition of the church.

First, the Bible teaches that the church is people, people who have been brought close to God at a great price. The writer of the book of

Hebrews after speaking of the sacrifice offered in former times with the blood of animals says, ". . . how much more shall the blood of Christ, who through the eternal Spirit offered himself without blemish to God, purify your conscience from dead works to serve the living God" (Hebrews 9:14). We have been brought near to God through Christ's blood shed on the cross. Paul put it this way: "Husbands, love your wives, as Christ loved the church and gave himself up for her . . . that he might present the church to himself in splendor, without spot or wrinkle or any such thing, that she might be holy and without blemish" (Ephesians 5:25–27). Those who are in the church know that the church is made up of men, and women, and children who together were brought to God at the price of the cross. Now, because of that cross, they can experience together His love, and acceptance, and power.

Second, the Bible teaches that the church has not only been brought to God at the price of the cross—the church is a family brought together at that same price. The church is unique because of its beginning. It was not formed so that there would be a separation between good and bad people, or to give reason for religious people to meet, or even to perform service to the world. The church was formed because a Man died on a cross to form it. To all people everywhere who have believed in Christ and what He has done on the cross, God gave the power to come into the family (John 1:12).

I once heard a man who had been rejected by his human family stand before a congregation and say, "I don't have a mother and father, or a sister or brother in the human sense anymore. But I do have a family. You are my family. Last week I had holes in my shoes and one of my brothers came to me and said, 'My brother should not have holes in his shoes,' and he bought me a new pair of shoes. I have been hungry and my sister has said, 'My brother should not be hungry,' and she gave me a meal. I have been afraid, and my family has said to me, 'Our brother should not be afraid because the family is with him,' and they comforted me. I don't have an earthly family anymore. But I have you, and you are really my family." That man defined the church.

But the church is not only a family, brought to God and to each other at the price of the cross. *Third,* the church is a family with a fantastic heritage. Paul said, "So then you are no longer strangers and sojourners, but you are fellow citizens with the saints and members of the household of God, built upon the foundation of apostles and prophets . . ." (Ephesians 2:19, 20). There is no other organization on the face of the earth with the heritage of the church. When Paul wrote the above words to the churches in Asia, he was writing to men and women of low estate. There were many slaves, and vassals, and common people. He was saying, "My brothers and sisters, you may not have a great family heritage, you may not have much prestige here, but you have something much greater. You are a part of a spiritual family whose roots go back thousands of years. You are a part of a family built of great men and women of God who, because they were committed to the family, and because many of them were strong and courageous, have given you a heritage you should never forget."

The church is a family with a great heritage brought to God and together at the price of a cross. But it is more than that. It is a family whose head is Jesus Christ. Paul said, "For the husband is the head of the wife as Christ is the head of the church, his body, and is himself its Savior" (Ephesians 5:23). The church is not a democracy. It is a dictatorship! Christ is the absolute Head. The church's responsibility is not to meet together and to decide what to do, or even to look at the problems in the world and decide which ones are to be ministered unto by the church. The church comes together to discern what Jesus wants to do, and to do it.

Christ is the Head of our family. The family is His responsibility. We hear a lot today about the demise of the church. That will never happen. Why? Because people who are a part of the church are so wise and courageous? No! Because the church belongs to Christ and He doesn't stand behind dying concerns.

Now we are prepared to deal with the central question: What difference does the church make? *First,* the church makes a difference because, as a Christian, you are incomplete without other Christians. The Bible says, "For the body does not consist of one member but of many. If all were a single organ, where would the body be? As it is, there are many parts, yet one body. The eye cannot say to the hand,

116

'I have no need of you,' nor again the head to the feet, 'I have no need of you.' If one member suffers, all suffer together; if one member is honored, all rejoice together. Now you are the body of Christ and individually members of it" (1 Corinthians 12:14, 19-21, 26, 27).

The forces of the world are angry, and consuming and strong. If you ever expect to stand for a minute you must stand with others. Without your brothers and sisters you will not last. When you are ridiculed you will cave in if you don't have someone who understands. When you are wounded by the arrows of the world you will die if you don't have anyone to bind up your wounds. When you are afraid because of the forces set against you, you will not make it if you don't have brothers and sisters to stand with you. The best way for a military leader to bring the arguments and divisions in his forces to an end is not to speak to the divisions and arguments, but to speak about the enemy. A Christian needs the church because without the church the Christian would be incomplete.

Second, the church makes a difference because it is only within fellowship that a Christian experiences the fullness of God. In the third chapter of Ephesians, the Apostle Paul is talking about the church as a unified fellowship where ". . . Christ may dwell in your hearts through faith; that you, being rooted and grounded in love, may have power to comprehend with all the saints what is the breadth and length and height and depth, and to know the love of Christ which surpasses knowledge, that you may be filled with all the fulness of God" (Ephesians 3:17–19). Jesus said that when two or three gathered together in His Name, He would be there (Matthew 18:20). A limb of a tree may be very beautiful. You may think it is so beautiful that you want to cut it off the tree and take it home and put it on your doorstep. But if you do that—if you detach it from the tree—that limb will die. So will you without the church.

Third, the church serves as a corrective to your faith. The church says to its individual members, "That which was from the beginning, which we have heard, which we have seen with our eyes, which we have looked upon and touched with our hands, concerning the word of life . . . we proclaim also to you . . ." (1 John 1:1, 3). One of my pet peeves is the person who sticks his nose in the air and says, "I have outgrown the church." That is much like a first year music student saying that he has outgrown Bach. The problem is not in Bach! History teaches that when organizations move outside the institution of the church (which contains and utilizes the Body of Christ) those organizations, more often than not, become one-sided or heretical. The church contains much wisdom, and experience, and knowledge. Only the very foolish or the very blind will spurn it.

Finally, the church is the instrument by which Christ accomplishes his purposes in the world. Just as mountain climbers scaling a high peak need one another in order to accomplish their goal, so the Christian needs other Christians if Christ's work is to be done. With the mountain climbers it is not a question of one making it and the others not making it. If they all don't, none of them will. It is the same with the church. In witnessing, and serving, and helping, and preaching, and loving, and caring, and changing, and inspiring, and feeding, and clothing, and healing, there is so much to do that only a fool would even attempt to begin without others. The church must act as a body. God's gifts (1 Corinthians 12) were not all poured out on one Christian. They were distributed among many. That which you can't do with that which God has given you, must be done with others whose gifts are different from yours. That includes almost everything Christ has sent us to do.

Now I want to add one final word of caution here. The Christian must be very careful about the individual church he or she chooses. There is much in our time which is labeled *church* which isn't. For instance, it is possible for a church to be so involved with the world that you can't tell the difference between it and the world. A church can become only another social service organization where good friends meet to do good in the community. There is nothing wrong with that, but it isn't the church. For instance, it is possible for the church to become nothing more than another gathering place for fun and games. There is nothing wrong with that either, but it isn't the church. For instance, it is possible for a church to go so far away from the teaching of the Bible that the Bible isn't important. That certainly is the prerogative of any group of people who are meeting together, but it isn't the church. For instance, it is possible for a church to turn in on itself caring only for its own needs. That is perfectly proper, but it isn't the church. There are a lot of churches which are peopled by honest and sincere members, but if the Scriptures are not taught, if Christ is not lifted up, if the church's mission is not taken seriously, then you ought to be very careful. No church is perfect but there are churches whose ministry will proclaim God's Word in such a fashion that you will want to go and proclaim it to the world. Search out that kind of church. Work for it. Reach out with it. Serve in it. Pray for it. And make sure that it is stronger because you are a part of it. You'll be glad you did!

14
When You Know the Future

"I am the Alpha and the Omega," says the Lord God, who is and who was and who is to come, the Almighty. REVELATION 1:8

When Lincoln Steffens returned from Russia in 1919 he said to Bernard Baruch, "I have been over into the future, and it works." That comment from the lips of Steffens was less than accurate. However, the same words, when spoken by a Christian, point to a reality known only to those who are in relationship to Jesus Christ. Joe Pagan and Jane Cynic think the future is a frightening spectrum of the unknowable. The scientist thinks the future is the product of undetermined causes. The philosopher thinks the future is only the subject for abstract discussion. But for the Christian the future is the exciting prospect of seeing Jesus Christ put it all together!

We watched a horror movie last night on television. As the tension mounted there was not a calm person in the room, except me. Everyone was frightened, except me. No one went to the kitchen to get refreshments, except me. Do you know why the horror movie didn't bother me? Because I had seen the movie before. I knew exactly what was going to happen. I knew the end, and because I did, the beginning and the middle were not nearly as frightening. The Christian has the same edge on the world. In the midst of fear, and crisis, and chaos, the Christian knows how the whole thing is going to turn out!

First, the Christian knows about the future of the world. The prophet Isaiah saw the future and spoke the Word of God, "For behold, I create new heavens and a new earth; and the former things shall not be remembered or come into mind" (Isaiah 65:17). The Bible points to God's purpose for the world: "But do not ignore this one fact, beloved, that with the Lord one day is as a thousand years, and a thousand years as one day. The Lord is not slow about His promise as some count slowness, but is forbearing toward you, not wishing that any should perish, but that all should reach repentance. But the day of the Lord will come like a thief, and then the heavens will pass away with a loud noise, and the elements will be dissolved with fire, and the earth and the works that are upon it will be burned up. But according to His promise we wait for new heavens and a new earth in which righteousness dwells" (2 Peter 3:8–10, 13).

Our world is in chaos. Never before has there been so much confusion, and because of the confusion, so much danger. Every paper screams out the message of a new crisis, a new problem, and a new fear. There is no hope for our world if one looks for hope within the bounds of our world. We just simply don't have enough solutions to go around. If air pollution doesn't strangle us, the population explosion will crowd us out. If we aren't starved to death because we can't produce enough food for the world, we will blow ourselves up because we can't produce enough understanding for the world. War, poverty, racism, pollution, march by like tin soldiers in review before the world. Most of us just go get a fresh six-pack and change the station.

The problem is that the most we can do is tinker with the mess. Education, psychology, and religion have done their best, but "educated" men built bombs, "adjusted" men turned away, and "religious" men just smile and talk about love. There was a time when some of us spoke about how the world was getting better and better in every way, every day. No sane man, who has taken the time to notice recently, would dare to make that kind of statement. Things aren't getting better; they are getting worse. Our bombs are more sophisticated, that's all. Our hate is more subtle, that's all. Our crosses aren't made of wood anymore, that's all.

But in the midst of all the chaos, and the crisis, and the fear, and the confusion, and the destruction, the Christian can stand sure in the knowledge that the Master has spoken, and He doesn't lie. "In the world you have tribulation; but be of good cheer, I have overcome the world" (John 16:33). Jesus is in control! He knows what He is doing! We can trust Him! Aren't you glad!

Second, the Christian knows the future of the family to which he belongs. "Now to him who by the power at work within us is able to do far more abundantly than all that we ask or think, to him be glory in the church and in Christ Jesus to all generations, for ever and ever. Amen" (Ephesians 3:20, 21). Jesus promised that even the gates of hell would not prevail against His church (Matthew 16:18). In other words, the church is going to last forever.

A man once told me that he would not become a Christian and support Christ's church because he didn't want to be a part of a dying institution. He didn't know what he was talking about, but he was in pretty good company. Caesar, Nero, Julian, Hitler, Stalin and a host of others have proclaimed the death of the church of Christ. They are all dead. The church isn't. The church is alive, not because it is made up of such good and wise men and women, not because the members of the church are so discerning, not because God picked the best people to be in the church. The church is alive and will continue to live because it is Christ's church and He won't let it die. He promised.

I have a German shepherd whose name is Barnabus. Barnabus bit the veterinarian the other day and it was not one of my happier moments. The vet had to give Barnabus two shots. Barnabus took the first shot surprisingly well. He didn't whine or try to move. But as the vet went back to the table to prepare the second shot, Barnabus watched him out of the corner of his eye. As the vet came back with the needle prepared, my dog seemed to be saying, "Buddy, I can take one of those, but you only get away with it once." And as the vet's hand moved toward Barnabus, Barnabus turned and, without warning, bit him. Someday, maybe soon, Jesus is coming back to our planet. His promise is that although He was humiliated once, we will only get away with it once. Man was able to do with God's Son what they willed the first time. He was beaten, and scorned, and hung on a cross.

That won't ever happen again. The next time it will be different. The next time Jesus comes back, He will come in power and glory, and He will come back to receive the church unto Himself. "For this we declare to you by the word of the Lord, that we who are alive, who are left until the coming of the Lord, shall not precede those who have fallen asleep. For the Lord himself will descend from heaven with a cry of command, with the archangel's call, and with the sound of the trumpet of God. And the dead in Christ will rise first; then we who are alive, who are left, shall be caught up together with them in the clouds to meet the Lord in the air; and so we shall always be with the Lord. Therefore comfort one another with these words" (1 Thessalonians 4:15–18). The church's future is secure. You can hang your hat on it!

Finally, and connected with the church's future, the Christian is sure of his own future. Jesus said, "Let not your hearts be troubled; believe in God, believe also in me. In my Father's house are many rooms; if it were not so, would I have told you that I go to prepare a place for you? And when I go and prepare a place for you, I will come again and will take you to myself, that where I am you may be also" (John 14:1–3). The Apostle Paul said, "So it is with the resurrection of the dead. What is sown is perishable, what is raised is imperishable. It is sown in dishonor, it is raised in glory. It is sown in weakness, it is raised in power. It is sown a physical body, it is raised a spiritual body" (1 Corinthians 15:42–44).

I have a friend who is a Christian and who often makes those traffic reports for a Boston radio station during the morning and afternoon "drive times." One time I was discussing with him the dangers of going up in a helicopter so many times. I mentioned to him that every time he went up in that helicopter he was increasing his chances of an accident. He smiled and said, "I don't worry much. If I come down, I will go up." He knows what he is talking about. Why? Because he has listened to the only Person who knows anything about death. He doesn't put his hope in a minister or priest. Ministers and priests will die too, and they don't know any more than he does. He doesn't put his hope in wishful thinking. Rose-colored glasses may make things look better but they don't make things better. My friend had put his faith in the only One who has died and come back to talk about it. Jesus said, ". . . because I live, you will live also" (John 14:19).

Dwight L. Moody knew what he was talking about: "Some day you will read in the papers that D.L. Moody of East Northfield, is dead. Don't you believe a word of it! At that moment I shall be more alive than I am now, I shall have gone up higher, that is all; out of this old clay tenement into a house that is immortal—a body that death cannot touch; that sin cannot taint; a body fashioned like unto His glorious body. I was born of the flesh in 1837. I was born of the Spirit in 1856. That which is born of the flesh may die. That which is born of the Spirit will live forever." Because Jesus promised, I am looking forward to meeting D.L. Moody someday. That will be one of the nice things about heaven.

Armed with the above facts, my brother and sister, you can now really live! Because you know the future, you don't ever have to be afraid of anything again. Jesus said, "So have no fear of them; for nothing is covered that will not be revealed, or hidden that will not be known. What I tell you in the dark, utter in the light; and what you hear whispered, proclaim upon the housetops. And do not fear those who kill the body but cannot kill the soul . . ." (Matthew 10:26–28). There is nothing, absolutely nothing, the world can do to you that will have any ultimate significance. At the dog track, the dogs are persuaded to do something as dumb as run around the track because they are convinced they will catch a mechanical rabbit which is always kept just so far in front of them as they run. Those dogs think they are scaring the mechanical rabbit. They think they will catch it. They may even think they will beat that rabbit around that track. But it will never happen because the man who runs the mechanical rabbit is always in control. The rabbit will always get to the finish line before the dogs. The Christian's life is like that mechanical rabbit. The world may think it will destroy, and hurt, and devour it, but it won't because Jesus is in control and the end is already decided.

Second, because the Christian knows the future, the Christian is free to spend His life for Christ with the knowledge that after this life is spent there will be much, much more. Jesus said, "Do not lay up for yourselves treasures on earth, where moth and rust consume and where thieves break in and steal, but lay up for yourselves treasures in heaven, where neither moth nor rust consumes and where thieves

125

do not break in and steal" (Matthew 6:19, 20). I do not envy Joe Pagan's fun. In fact, I believe that if he is wise, he will eat, and drink, and be merry, that he will hustle for as much as he can as fast as he can. That is all he has. If he doesn't get it here, he won't ever get it. Had Christ not promised me eternal life, I would be right in there with him. But, you see, the vastness of eternity insures me all of the time in the world. I will use all of that time as Christ has asked, secure in the knowledge that none of it will be wasted, that all of my efforts will be in the service of a cause which will last forever. Death gives significance to life in different ways for the Christian and for the non-Christian. The non-Christian, aware of his death, will make every moment of life count for self. The Christian, aware of his death, will make every moment of life count for Christ.

Third, because I know the facts in the matter, I can relax about the future. Because Jesus said that He had overcome the world, I don't have to worry anymore. Tomorrow, when my neighbor picks up the morning paper, reads about another crisis, and falls apart, I can smile because I know how this whole thing is going to turn out. Jesus said, "Therefore I tell you, do not be anxious about your life . . ." (Matthew 6:25). If I had nothing to go by, except the morning paper, or the wisdom of the politicians, or the strength of the United Nations, that statement would be ridiculous. I would be very anxious about my life, and with very good reason. But Jesus didn't just tell me not to be anxious about my life, He told me why and that makes a lot of difference.

Finally, because I know the facts about the future, it is important that I share what I know with others. If I had a cure for a terrible disease, what kind of person would I be if I didn't share that cure with the world? Well, I have something better than a cure for disease, and so do you! It is knowledge about the future, and how wonderful it will be for those who know Christ. It is the knowledge that, considering the vastness of eternity, even disease is not that important, for, "Then I saw a new heaven and a new earth; for the first heaven and the first earth had passed away, and the sea was no more. And I saw the holy city, new Jerusalem, coming down out of heaven from God, prepared as a bride adorned for her husband; and I heard a great voice from the throne saying, 'Behold, the dwelling of God is with men. He will dwell with them, and they shall be his people, and God himself will be with them; he will wipe away every tear from their eyes, and death shall be no more, neither shall there be mourning nor crying nor pain any more, for the former things have passed away' "(Revelation 21:1–4).

Let me again, my brother and sister, welcome you into our family. You have found a very good thing. Now go and tell someone about it!